Suzanne McNeill's

50 BEST

Scrap Happy

FABRIC TREASURES

Leisure Arts, Inc.
and
Oxmoor House, Inc.

Dedicated to my mother, Lois Alexander Browne. As a toddler I watched my mother cut fabric into strips and hook this 9' x 12' rug by hand. When I was a teenager, our family enjoyed the beautiful floral rug as the centerpiece in our home.

Printed in the United States of America
First Printing

Library of Congress
Catalog Card
Number 98-75105

Hardcover
ISBN 1-57486-150-6

Softcover
ISBN 1-57486-149-2

Leisure Arts, Inc.
P.O. Box 55595
Little Rock, AR 7221

Table of Contents

*S*craps of fabric and bits of 'This and That' are the supplies that my mother and grandmother used when they taught me to stitch and sew. During the depression, my mother never discarded an entire piece of clothing. That would be considered a waste, and my mother's motto was "Waste not, want not".

In our home the custom was to cut out the zippers, to clip off the buttons, to remove any decoration and to "rip" the fabric into strips. Then, each little treasure was neatly filed away in a collection of cigar boxes to await its opportunity for reuse.

This book began when I was a toddler. I watched in amazement as my mother ripped old wool suits into strips to hook a room size rug for our family room. Next, my great grandmother taught me to use scraps to make embroidered napkins, rag dolls, personalized gifts, little quilts and rag rugs with fabrics from outgrown clothing.

As a homemaker I developed an original technique for stitching durable rag rugs with strips of fabric. *Family Circle* magazine pictured two of my rug designs on their cover and published an article showing how to make the rugs. **Design Originals** published dozens of rug patterns, books and kits. I also developed a technique for making rag baskets with strips of fabric by wrapping and coiling the strips around rope. I traveled the country teaching people how to make rugs and baskets.

Your scrap collection can easily be developed into a wide variety of subjects. In ScrapHappy you'll see how easy it is to make simple rag balls from strips of fabric, and how to turn those balls into darling Rag-Muffin dolls. You can also turn a scrap collection into rag rugs, little quilts, welcome mats, dolls and ornaments.

Whenever possible, I use notions and materials that were part of my personal family history and I encourage you to do the same. If I don't have enough, it is always fun to look for odds and ends at a flea market or tag sale.

Enjoy these projects and use this book as a valuable resource for years to come.

Suzanne

Basic Instructions for Small Stuff

Stack Fabrics - Stack 2 layers of cotton quilt batting. Fold fabric with the right sides together, then stack it on top of the batting.

Transfer Patterns Trace the pattern, transfer to cardboard and cut out. Place the cardboard pattern on the fabric and trace around the pattern with a disappearing pen.

Stitch Layers - Machine stitch along the traced lines, stitching through both layers of batting and both layers of fabric. Leave the seam openings unstitched.

Cut Out Shapes - Cut the shapes out 1/4" from the stitched lines. Clip the curves and trim the corners.

Turn and Stuff - Turn right side out through the opening. (If no opening is indicated, cut a slit in backing fabric, then turn right side out through the slit.) Stuff item, then sew slit closed.

Stitch Details - Embroider facial features. Add 'blush' to cheeks with a swab stick. Use hot glue to add details with floss, buttons, fabric and/or beads. Optional: Tea dye item, see page 46.

This 'n That

For generations, mothers have been teaching daughters to sew. In colonial times, early American women mostly sewed out of necessity and then later on for pleasure.

Needlework took two forms, "plain" and "fancy". Plain sewing was considered essential for stitching ordinary clothing and linens, such as sheets, towels and bedcoverings. Simple stitches like the back, whip, running and cross stitches were used.

Fancy needlework was saved for purely decorative work. Most often it was done by a privileged woman who had time to indulge at her leisure. Museum quality needlework that has survived the ages is usually fancy work since these were the cherished mementos, passed down through generations. Conversely, plain work was used, reused, cut down and remodeled, until only the scraps remained.

Scraps were often the materials that were used. During the depression, families never discarded a piece of clothing. That would be considered a waste, and the motto was "Waste not, want not". The rule was to cut out zippers, clip off buttons, dismantle any decoration and "rip" fabric into strips. Then, each notion was neatly filed away in a marked envelope, a protective bag or a color coordinated box to await its opportunity for reuse.

With these scraps women made small stuff... a little of this and a little of that. Sewing with simple stitches, it was quick and easy to make rag balls, ornaments, stuffed hearts, garlands, trinkets and charming dolls.

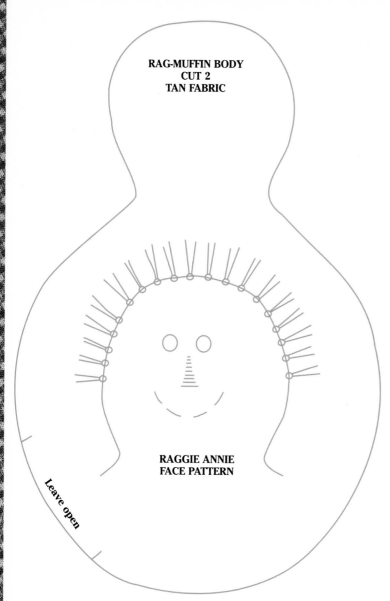

**RAG-MUFFIN BODY
CUT 2
TAN FABRIC**

Leave open

**RAGGIE ANNIE
FACE PATTERN**

**DOLLY
FACE PATTERN**

'Gingersnap' with Snaps for Ha[...]

MATERIALS:

Tan fabric • ½" strips of assorted print fabrics • 2 Black [...]
beads • Red and Brown Embroidery floss • 8 snaps • 4 but[...]
tons • Polyester fiberfill

INSTRUCTIONS:

Make a Rag-Muffin body. Using 3 strands of floss, make a[...]
back stitch Red mouth and straight stitch Brown nose.
Stitch buttons and beads for eye, snaps for hair. Wrap doll with[...]
assorted fabric strips. Glue 2 buttons on the front of dress.

'Raggie Annie' with a Big Hear[...]

MATERIALS:

Tan fabric • ½" strips of assorted print fabrics • 2 Black [...]
beads • Red and Brown embroidery floss • Red acrylic
paint • Wood heart • Polyester fiberfill

INSTRUCTIONS:

Make a Rag-Muffin body. Using 3 strands of Red floss, make[...]
a running stitch mouth and a straight stitch nose. Using 6[...]
strands of Brown floss, sew hair along head seam. Wrap doll[...]
with fabric strips. Paint the heart Red, sand the edges then[...]
hot glue to front of doll.

Buddy Boy with a Paper Hat is a Joy

MATERIALS:

Gold print fabric • Brown print fabric • ½" strips of assorted print fabrics • One
¾" and four ½" Navy Blue buttons • Black Embroidery floss • Piece of newspaper • Polyester fiberfill

INSTRUCTIONS:

Make a Rag-Muffin body. Using 3 strands of Black floss, make a back stitch mouth.
Glue buttons for eyes. Wrap doll with fabric strips using a contrasting strip for
the belt. Stitch 2 buttons on the front of shirt and stitch one button on the belt.
Make a hat from newspaper. Use a safety pin to secure the hat on Buddy's head.

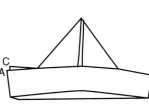

**BUDDY
FACE PATTERN**

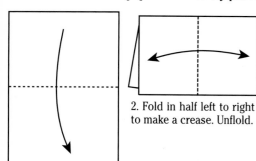

1. Cut a 3½" x 4½" piece of paper.
Fold in half from top to bottom.

2. Fold in half left to right
to make a crease. Unflold.

3. Fold corners E and F to the
center crease.

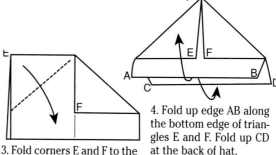

4. Fold up edge AB along
the bottom edge of trian-
gles E and F. Fold up CD
at the back of hat.

5. Place hat on doll. Secure on
the back with a safety pin.

Rag-Muffins

A ball of scraps holds
a token of love.
Create meaningful little rag
dolls from scraps of fabric and
outgrown clothing. Decorate
their faces and clothes with
buttons, snaps and floss.

Rag-Muffin Body - Trace, sew, cut out and stuff the body, see page 6. Add facial features...blush, eyes and mouth.

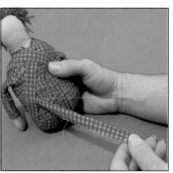

Wrap Body - Rip fabric into 1/2" wide strips. Wrap the body, slowly turning the doll as you cover all areas. Optional: Add small arms.

Rag Basket

In Mexico and Haiti, fabric scraps are salvaged to weave into colorful baskets. A sturdy reed or rope core lends its usefulness and natural beauty to the shape. Create a basket the size and shape you like and add handles to the basket by simply guiding the rope core to the desired shape.

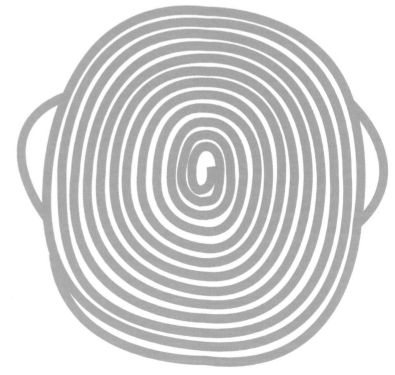

RAG BASKET DIAGRAM

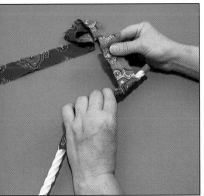

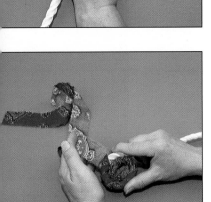

Rag Baskets

Note: Pull the wraps, especially the Joining Wraps, very tight. Wrap all Joining Wraps twice.

Basic Materials:
You'll need 1/2" to 3/4" thick basket coiling or rope, a large needle, fabric remnants cut or ripped into 1" x 44" strips and scissors.

Begin the Coil - Taper one end of the coiling. Thread a fabric strip onto the needle. Begin to wind the strip around the coil about 4" from the end... winding toward the end. Overlap the first wrap to hold it firm. Wrap almost to the end. Bend the coil to make a loop.

Always Wrap Tight - Continue to wrap until the loop is secure. Push needle through the center. Bend the coil to form a continuous circle. **Wrap strip** around the coil 3 times, then **Join** it by bringing it into the center twice. Repeat for three continuous rows.

Joining Stitches - Keep strips flat as you wrap so the strips will cover as much coiling as possible.

Bottom - As you begin the basket, wrap coils in a flat shape until the bottom is as large as you want.

Shape the Sides - When the bottom is large enough, add shape by bringing the coils up on the sides. To end a basket, taper the end of coiling. Wrap until the last coil joins the basket edge smoothly. Tip: To make the basket stronger, use two pieces of coiling in the top row.

Optional Handles - As you wrap the top row of coiling, pull one piece of coiling out on each side and wrap it separately to form handles. Secure the end of the last fabric strip between coils with glue.

Rag Balls

Thrifty homemakers have wound scraps of fabric into rag balls for centuries. Make a collection of colorful balls to create nostalgic home decor.

Basic Materials:
You'll need 1/4 yard of 44" wide fabric (or 10 continuous yards of 1" wide rag strips) and a 20" x 27" sheet of newspaper (or a 3" styrofoam ball)

Finished Size: - 3"

Fabric Strips - Rip or cut fabric into 1" x 44" strips. Tie the ends of all the strips together to make a continuous strip about 10 yards long.

Make the Ball - Wad the sheet of newspaper up into a tight ball. Wrap the 10 yard long strip around the ball alternating sides until the newspaper is completely covered. Tuck the end of the last strip under.

'Have a Heart' Pin Cushions

Pin cushions have long been household necessities as well as attractive gifts.

**ANNA HEAD PATTERN
CUT 2
TAN FLANNEL**

**ANNA WING PATTERN
CUT 2 MUSLIN**

7¼"

3"

**ANNA PATCHWORK DIAGRAM
TO BE PATCHED ON TOP ON
ONE MUSLIN WING**

**ANNA STAR PATTERN
CUT 1
BROWN PAPER**

See the
pattern
for the
Pumpkin
Heart on
page 16.

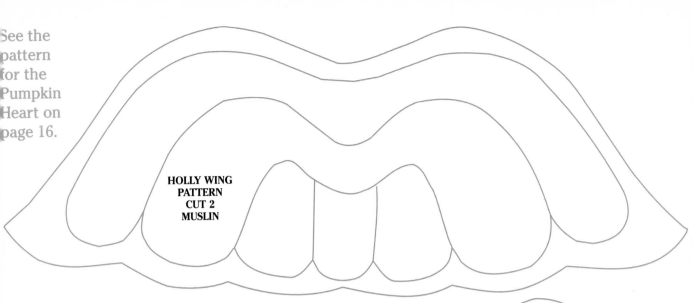

HOLLY WING
PATTERN
CUT 2
MUSLIN

Holly the Girl with a Blue Heart

MATERIALS: Fabric (Muslin for head and wings, Blue print for body, ¾" x 12" Navy/Tan check for bow) • Warm & Natural batting • Polyester fiberfill • Blonde doll hair • Black permanent marker • Cosmetic blush • Cotton swab • Red, Flesh, Metallic Gold acrylic paint • Fine Gold thread

INSTRUCTIONS:

Using the patterns, cut two wings and two heads from muslin. Cut two heart bodies from Blue print. Make the head. Paint the head Flesh and the mouth Red. Draw the eyes and nose with the marker and rub blush on the cheeks. Glue the hair on the head. Sew around the heart body, cut out.

Cut a slit in the back of the heart, turn right side out, stuff and sew the opening closed. Glue the head on the top of the heart. Tie a bow around the body.

Make the wings then machine stitch along the inside lines to give a quilted effect. Paint the wings with Metallic Gold, let dry. Sew or glue wings to the back of the body. Sew the ends of the thread to the wings for a hanger, knot to secure.

Anna with Patchwork Wings

MATERIALS: Fabric (Tan flannel for head and body, Muslin for back of wings, 1" strips of prints for patchwork wings) • Black doll hair • Warm & Natural batting • Polyester fiberfill • Black permanent marker • Cosmetic blush • Cotton swab • Red and Metallic Gold acrylic paint • Fine Gold thread • 2" square of Brown paper

INSTRUCTIONS:

Using the patterns, cut two wings from muslin, two heart bodies and two heads from flannel. Paint the mouth Red. Make the head. Make the heart body. Draw the eyes and nose with the marker and rub blush on the cheeks. Glue hair on the head then glue the head on the body.

Referring to the photo and diagram, sew strips of fabric to one piece of muslin wings to make patchwork for the wings front. Stack the muslin wing back, the patchwork wing front and a layer of batting. Make the wings then machine stitch along the patchwork seams with Gold thread.

Assemble the doll. Cut the star from the Brown paper then paint it Metallic Gold and glue on the head. Sew the ends of the thread to the wings for a hanger, knot to secure.

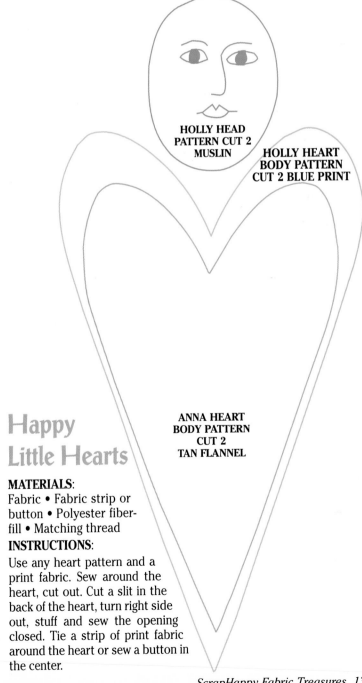

HOLLY HEAD
PATTERN CUT 2
MUSLIN

HOLLY HEART
BODY PATTERN
CUT 2 BLUE PRINT

ANNA HEART
BODY PATTERN
CUT 2
TAN FLANNEL

Happy Little Hearts

MATERIALS:
Fabric • Fabric strip or button • Polyester fiberfill • Matching thread

INSTRUCTIONS:

Use any heart pattern and a print fabric. Sew around the heart, cut out. Cut a slit in the back of the heart, turn right side out, stuff and sew the opening closed. Tie a strip of print fabric around the heart or sew a button in the center.

Christmas Stars Garland

Hanging stars are cut free hand and stitched with folk art accents.

FABRIC: 4" square of Tan flannel for head • 6" square of Red/Tan check for heart • ¼ yard of muslin • Two ¾" x 27" strips of Tan/Green plaid • Tan felt

MATERIALS: Polyester fiberfill • Batting • Embroidery floss (Tan, Black, Red) • ¾" Gold button • 4" of pine greenery • Berry Red and Raw Sienna acrylic paint

INSTRUCTIONS:

Trace the patterns.

Head - Transfer the head pattern to a double layer of flannel. Sew around the head, cut out. Cut a slit in the back of the head, turn right side out, stuff and sew the opening closed.

French knot eyes and straight stitch nose with Tan floss. Make a straight stitch mouth with Red floss.

Twist greenery into a circle then glue it on the head for a halo.

Heart Body - Transfer the pattern to a double layer of Red/Tan fabric. Sew around the heart, then cut out. Cut a slit in the back of the heart, turn right side out, stuff and sew the opening closed. Glue the head on the top of the heart. Sew a button on the front.

Stars - Place batting under a double layer of muslin. Trace one large and two small star patterns. Sew around the stars, cut out. Cut a slit through one layer of the muslin, turn right side out, iron and sew the opening closed.

Paint the stars Berry Red. Thin Raw Sienna with water, paint the stars again.

Cut 3 center stars from felt. Blanket stitch around the edges then glue ends of floss to the back. Glue the felt stars on the painted stars. Glue the angel on the large star. Sew the stars together using Red floss. Sew the centers of the Green plaid strips to the end stars, tie the ends in bows.

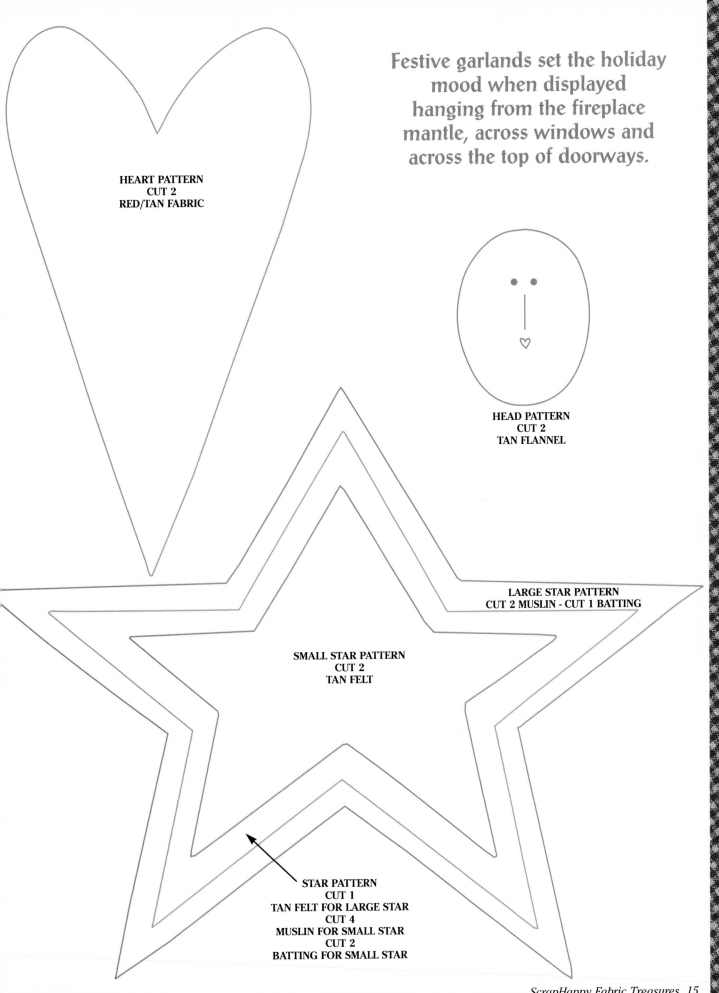

HEART PATTERN
CUT 2
RED/TAN FABRIC

Festive garlands set the holiday
mood when displayed
hanging from the fireplace
mantle, across windows and
across the top of doorways.

HEAD PATTERN
CUT 2
TAN FLANNEL

LARGE STAR PATTERN
CUT 2 MUSLIN - CUT 1 BATTING

SMALL STAR PATTERN
CUT 2
TAN FELT

STAR PATTERN
CUT 1
TAN FELT FOR LARGE STAR
CUT 4
MUSLIN FOR SMALL STAR
CUT 2
BATTING FOR SMALL STAR

FACE PATTERN

**HEART BODY PATTERN
CUT 2
TAN FLANNEL**

Pumpkins Have Hearts, Too

PICTURED ON PAGE 12

MATERIALS: 6" x 10" piece of Tan flannel • Papier mâché • 1" styrofoam ball • Pieces of grapevine wreath • Spanish moss • Black embroidery floss • ¾" Black button • Burnt Orange and Black acrylic paint • Polyester fiberfill

INSTRUCTIONS:

Trace the pattern pieces, transfer to cardboard and cut out.

Body & Head - Fold flannel with right sides together and trace the heart pattern. The traced line is the sewing line. Sew along traced line. Next cut out around the heart leaving a ¼" seam allowance. Make a slit in the back layer and turn right side out. Stuff the heart with fiberfill.

Transfer the embroidery pattern and backstitch the web with Black using the opening in the back to tie the knots. Sew a button on the spider. Hand stitch the opening closed.

Head - Paint the styrofoam ball Burnt Orange for the head. Paint the features Black. Glue the head on the body. Glue moss on the head for hair.

Wings - Soak grapevine pieces in water for one hour, shape into wings. Tie in the center, let dry. Glue the wings to the back of the body. Make a hanger with the Black floss.

Snowman Purse

MATERIALS: 6½" x 21" piece of Dark Green/Black stripe fabric • 6½" x 7½" piece of Warm & Natural batting • One yard of 3mm Black twisted cord • 1" button • Embroidery floss (Gold, Black, Dark Red, Tan) • Spray bottle • Tea dye

INSTRUCTIONS:

Batting - Tea dye the batting with a spray bottle, let dry.

Snowman - Transfer the snowman pattern to batting. Embroider the snowman outline Tan and the wings Gold using running stitches. French knot the eyes and mouth and straight stitch the scarf Black. Back stitch the nose Gold. Make the hearts with 2 loose Dark Red straight stitches couching the top of the stitches to form a heart.

Purse - Fold the Green/Black fabric in half lengthwise with wrong sides together, sew 2½" on each side of one end for the flap and turn right side out.

Make a buttonhole in the center of the flap. With right sides facing, sew the batting front to fabric, trim the corners and turn right side out. Glue the ends of the cord in the seams on each side to make the handle. Sew the button in place.

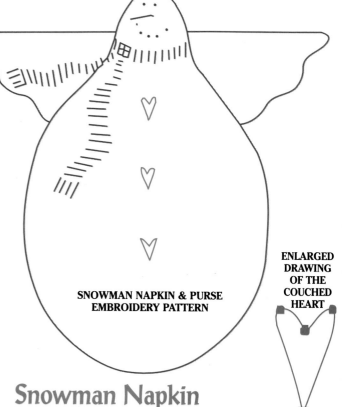

**SNOWMAN NAPKIN & PURSE
EMBROIDERY PATTERN**

**ENLARGED
DRAWING
OF THE
COUCHED
HEART**

Snowman Napkin

MATERIALS: 15" square of Warm & Natural batting • Embroidery floss (Gold, Black, Dark Red, Tan) • Spray bottle • Tea dye

INSTRUCTIONS:

Batting - Tea dye the batting with a spray bottle, let dry.

Snowman - Transfer the snowman pattern to batting. Embroider the snowman outline Tan and the wings Gold using running stitches. French knot the eyes and mouth and straight stitch the scarf Black. Back stitch the nose Gold. Make the hearts with 2 loose Dark Red straight stitches couching the top of the stitches to form a heart.

Running stitch around the napkin 1" from edge with Dark Red.

Mini Tree Necklace

MATERIALS: 4" square of Black felt • Small Gold bead with a loop • Moss Green and Burgundy embroidery floss • Pinking shears

INSTRUCTIONS:

Transfer the patterns to Black felt and cut out using pinking shears for the back piece. Straight stitch the tree Moss Green and the base Burgundy. Sew the front on the back leaving the top open.

Cut three 36" pieces of Moss Green floss. Tie together on one end and braid. Tie the ends together with an overhand knot to make the strap. Center and sew the strap to the inside of the flap with small stitches. Sew the bead on the front and cut a slit in the flap to fit over the bead.

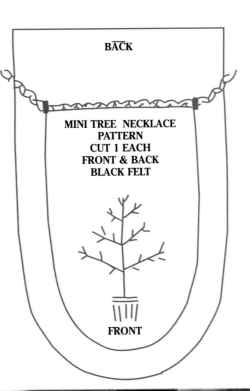

BACK

MINI TREE NECKLACE
PATTERN
CUT 1 EACH
FRONT & BACK
BLACK FELT

FRONT

Little Heartfelt Stitched Pieces

Ornamental needlework has been considered an art form for ages. Here a simple running stitch makes all the difference.

Ornament

MATERIALS:

1½" grapevine wreath • 9" of ¼" Gold ribbon • Iridescent glitter • White craft glue • Fine Gold thread

INSTRUCTIONS:

Cut a 1" by 12" strip of flannel for the scarf. Using the large patterns cut out and assemble the snowman. Make a curved line with glue down the front of the body, sprinkle with the glitter. Tie a ribbon bow and glue on the wreath. Glue the wreath on one end of the scarf. Sew ends of thread to the wings for a hanger, knot to secure.

**GARLAND BODY PATTERN
CUT 2 BATTING**

**PIN BODY PATTERN
CUT 2 BATTING**

**GARLAND WINGS
CUT 2 MUSLIN
CUT 1 BATTING**

**PIN HEAD
PATTERN
CUT 2
BATTING**

Snow Pin

MATERIALS:

1¼" pin back • scrap of batting

INSTRUCTIONS:

Cut a ½" x 6" strip of the flannel. Using the pin patterns, cut out and assemble the snowman. Glue the pin back on the wings.

Snow white hearts are winged in gold dust and elegantly hung on a rich green garland.

'Let It Snow' Snowmen

Basic Materials and Instructions

BASIC MATERIALS: Warm & Natural batting for body • Muslin for wings • Black flannel for scarf • Batting for wings • Polyester fiberfill • Gold craft wire • Gold embroidery floss • Peppercorns • Spray bottle • Tea dye • Hot glue • Cardboard • Metallic Antique Gold and Black acrylic paint • Black fine-tip permanent marker

BASIC INSTRUCTIONS:

Trace the pattern pieces, transfer to cardboard and cut out.

Heart Body & Head

Tea dye the batting with a spray bottle, let dry. Fold the batting with right sides together. Trace the heart and head patterns on the batting. The traced line is the sewing line. Sew along the traced line, cut out leaving a 1/4" seam allowance, make slits in the back layers and turn right side out. Stuff the hearts and heads with fiberfill. Hand stitch the slits closed.

Wings

Fold the muslin with right sides together and place on a thin layer of batting. Trace the wing pattern on the muslin and sew along the traced line, cut out leaving a 1/4" seam allowance, make a slit in the front layer and turn right side out. Transfer the design and machine stitch. Paint the wings Metallic Antique Gold. Trace over the stitching lines with thinned Black paint.

Assemble

Glue the head on the body and tie the scarf around the neck. Glue sides of the head to the heart. Embroider the nose Gold using straight stitches. Make the eyes and mouth with peppercorns or dot with Black permanent marker. Glue peppercorns for the buttons. Make the halo with the Gold craft wire. Glue the halo to the center of the wings and the wings to the back of the body.

LARGE HEART BODY
CUT 2
BATTING

HALO
PATTERN

Snowmen Garland

MATERIALS: Three 1¼" x 72" strips of Green check fabric • Two 1¼" x 25" strips of Gold plaid fabric • Green thread

INSTRUCTIONS:

Cut three ½" x 8" strips of flannel. Using the garland patterns, cut out and assemble three snowmen. Braid the Green fabric strips together and knot ends to secure.

Tie the Gold strips in a bow around the ends of the garland. Sew the snowmen on the garland using the Green thread.

GARLAND HEAD
PATTERN
CUT 2 BATTING

LARGE HEAD
PATTERN
CUT 2 BATTING

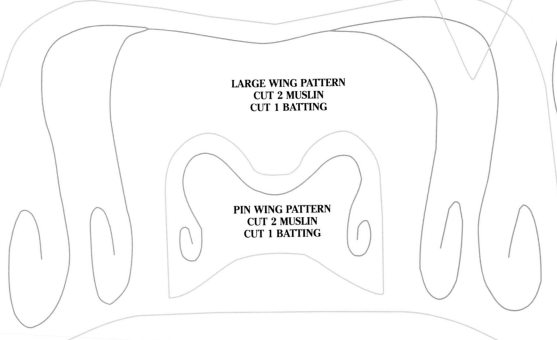

LARGE WING PATTERN
CUT 2 MUSLIN
CUT 1 BATTING

PIN WING PATTERN
CUT 2 MUSLIN
CUT 1 BATTING

SMALL HEAD
PATTERN
CUT 2 BATTING

Frosties of All Sizes

Basic Materials and Instructions

BASIC MATERIALS: Warm & Natural batting for body • Polyester fiberfill • Gold embroidery floss • Spray bottle • Tea dye • Twigs • Hot glue • Doll pellets • Black permanent marker • Cosmetic blush • Cotton swab • Cardboard

BASIC INSTRUCTIONS:
Trace the pattern pieces, transfer to cardboard and cut out. Tea dye the batting with a spray bottle, let dry. Fold the batting with right sides together. Trace body pattern on the batting. The traced line is the sewing line. Sew along the traced line and cut out leaving a ¼" seam allowance.

To make a box shaped bottom, fold the side seams together and sew ⅜" from the corners. Turn right side out. Fill the bottom with pellets and stuff the rest of the body with fiberfill. Hand stitch the opening closed. Dot the eyes and mouth with the marker. Straight stitch nose Gold. Rub blush on the cheeks. Cut small holes in back for the arms. Glue twigs in holes.

Small Frostie with Tree

MATERIALS: 2" grapevine wreath • Two 3" twigs • Plumosus • Iridescent glitter • White craft glue

INSTRUCTIONS:
Make the snowman. Cut a piece of plumosus. Glue on the front with thinned craft glue and sprinkle with glitter. Glue the bottom of the snowman in a wreath.

Frosties with Jackets

MATERIALS: Black/Tan check flannel • Scraps of Black felt • Two ½" White buttons • Red embroidery floss • Four 3" twigs • Two peppercorns

INSTRUCTIONS:
Make 2 snowmen. Cut 2 fronts and one back piece for each jacket from the flannel and the pockets from the felt. Blanket stitch the pockets to the large jacket with Red floss.

Glue pockets on the small jacket. Sew jacket side seams. Place jackets on the snowmen, glue the fronts together, turn down and glue the collars. Glue buttons to the large jacket and glue peppercorns to the small jacket.

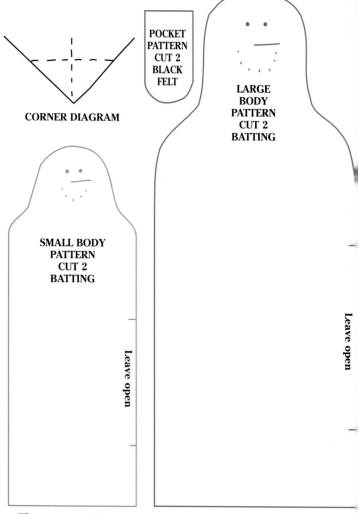

CORNER DIAGRAM

POCKET PATTERN CUT 2 BLACK FELT

LARGE BODY PATTERN CUT 2 BATTING

SMALL BODY PATTERN CUT 2 BATTING

Leave open

Leave open

Frostie Trio

MATERIALS: Three 3" grapevine wreaths • Three ¾" x 12" strips of Black flannel for scarves • Plumosus • White craft glue • Four 3" twigs • Iridescent glitter

INSTRUCTIONS: Make the snowmen with connecting twig arms. Cut pieces of plumosus. Glue on the fronts with thinned craft glue and sprinkle with glitter. Glue the bottoms of the snowmen in the wreaths. Tie the flannel around the necks for scarves.

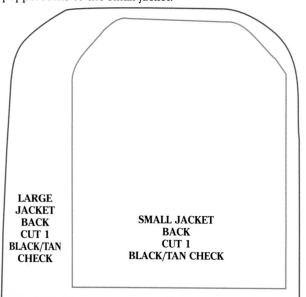

LARGE JACKET BACK CUT 1 BLACK/TAN CHECK

SMALL JACKET BACK CUT 1 BLACK/TAN CHECK

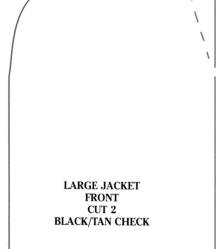

LARGE JACKET FRONT CUT 2 BLACK/TAN CHECK

SMALL JACKET FRONT CUT 2 BLACK/TAN CHECK

Fun Little Frosties to Cheer the Holidays

Mother Nature was the inspiration behind these primitive snowmen with green ferns and wooden twigs.

Button Box Treasure

A treasure trove collection of big buttons, black buttons, blue buttons... a big bunch of left-over buttons decorate the wings and coiled wire on this charming little doll.

Coiled Wire Hanger

You'll need 18 gauge craft wire to make the clever hanger.

Coiled Wire - Coil wire around a pen or pencil. Wind it around the pencil evenly. Gently remove wire coil from the pencil, then spread the coil as desired. Attach hanger to the wings then add buttons as an accent.

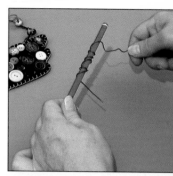

HEAD PATTERN
CUT 2
MUSLIN

Leave open

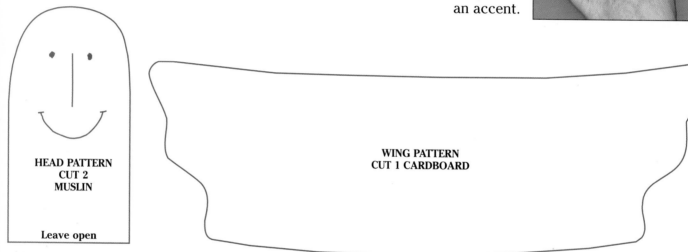

WING PATTERN
CUT 1 CARDBOARD

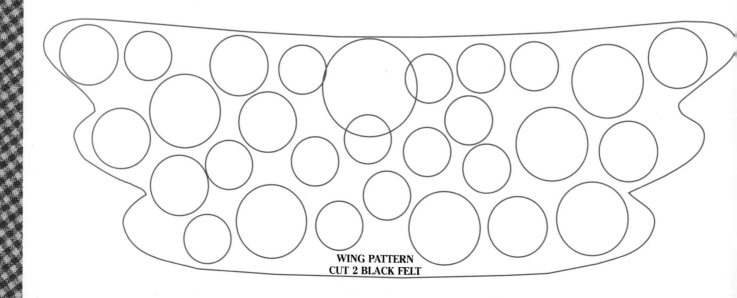

WING PATTERN
CUT 2 BLACK FELT

Where's My Button?

MATERIALS: 4" square of muslin for head • 6" x 8" piece of black felt for wings • Embroidery floss (Red, Black, Tan, Ecru) • Blonde curly wool doll hair • One large Gold and 33 assorted buttons • 13" of 18 gauge craft wire • Cosmetic blush • Cotton swab • Polyester fiberfill • 3" x 8" piece of cardboard

INSTRUCTIONS:

Trace the patterns.

Head - Trace the head pattern on a double layer of muslin. Sew around the head leaving an opening. Cut out, clip the curves and turn right side out. Stuff the head then hand stitch the opening closed.

Wings - Trace the pattern and cut 2 wings from felt and one smaller wing from cardboard. Sandwich the cardboard between the felt wings. Insert the head in the wings and stitch or glue the pieces together. Blanket stitch around the edges of the wings with Ecru floss.

Face - French knot eyes and straight stitch nose with Tan floss. Back stitch the mouth with Red floss. Rub blush on the cheeks and glue a 4" piece of hair on the head.

Hanger - Make holes in the wings 1½" from the ends. Coil the center of the wire. Insert one end of the wire in one hole, twist to secure. Secure the end in the other hole. Cut 24" of Black floss and fold in half. Thread 6 buttons on the floss and loosely twist the floss around the hanger. Glue the buttons to the wire and the end of the floss to the back of the wings to secure.

Buttons - Glue the remaining buttons on the wings with the large Gold button at the neck.

Small Winter Home   *by Rochelle Norris*

MATERIALS:

Two 2¾" x 3" wood dome cut outs for roof • ¼ yard of Green fabric • 5" x 8" piece of fusible web • Polyester fiberfill • Spanish moss • 4 sticks • Red mushroom bird • Jute • Silk pine greens • Pine cones • Burnt Umber and White DecoArt acrylic paint

INSTRUCTIONS:

Birdhouse - Make the birdhouse.

Roof - Paint the roof Burnt Umber. Glue the roof to top of the birdhouse with the bottom edges touching. Cut 7" of jute, glue the ends together to make loop and place in the roof gap. Thread the stick through the jute loop, glue the stick in place. Glue sticks under the roofline. Glue moss to the point on the front and 2 sticks under the roofline on the back of the house.

Trim - Glue a small clump of moss to the top of the roof. Glue the pine greens, pine cone and bird in place. Make a hole in birdhouse for the perch, glue a stick in the hole.

Fabric Birdhouse Instructions

1. Iron fusible web to the back of the birdhouse fabric. Peel off the backing and place muslin over the top, fuse together. Pin the pattern pieces on the fabric, cut out.

2. Fold down the seam allowance on one end of the torn strip and position at top of the house with right sides together. Sew the strip around front of the house. Reinforce the stitches at the beginning and end. Fold down the seam allowance on the strip at the opposite end before finishing. Clip the corners. Repeat for the back of the birdhouse.

3. Turn right side out and stuff firmly. Hand stitch the opening closed.

4. Optional: Use scissors to cut a small opening in the center front of the house for a perch. Cut a 2" to 3" stick. Glue the stick in hole for the perch.

5. Decorate the birdhouse following the individual project instructions.

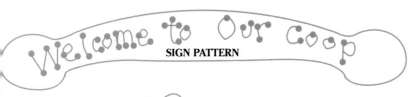

SIGN PATTERN

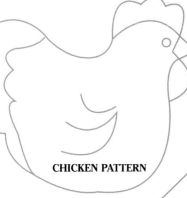

CHICKEN PATTERN

Soft Birdhouses

Gathered fabric scraps and bits of this and that are nested together to make a soft sided birdhouse.

**WINTER HOME
FRONT & BACK
PATTERN
CUT 2**

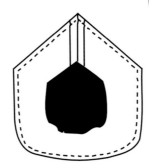

**SEW STRIPS OF FABRIC ON
FRONT AND BACK OF
BIRDHOUSE FOR SIDES.**

'Welcome to Our Coop' Large Red House

by Rochelle Norris

FABRIC: 9½" x 16" piece of Red fabric • 5" x 25" torn strip of Red • 9½" x 16" piece of muslin
DECOART ACRYLIC PAINT: Black • Rookwood Red • Raw Sienna • Antique Gold
MATERIALS:
2 wood shingles cut to 5" x 6" and 5" x 5¾" • 9½" x 16" piece of fusible web • Polyester fiberfill •
2 large chicken cut outs • Wood rocker • Spanish moss • Sticks • 24" of 18 gauge craft wire • 5 mini
eggs • Jute • .01 Black pen • Natural raffia
INSTRUCTIONS:
Birdhouse - Make the birdhouse.
Roof - Drill 2 holes in each shingle 1½" from the sides and ¼" from the edge. Overlap the ends and wire together, coil the wire ends. Glue roof on top of the house. Glue 2 large sticks to the front of the birdhouse under the roof. Glue moss under the roof on the back of the house.
Trim - Glue small clump of moss to the point of the house. Place small sticks together referring to photo, tie at the corners with jute. Glue moss on the bottom stick.
Chickens - Paint the chickens Raw Sienna with Rookwood Red accents. Paint the beaks Antique Gold and dot the eyes Black. Draw the wings with pen. Glue the chickens and eggs in place.
Sign - Write 'Welcome to Our Coop' on the rocker, make the dots on letters and glue in place.
Finish - Tie a raffia bow on the hanger.

**WELCOME TO OUR COOP
FRONT & BACK
PATTERN
CUT 2**

Basic Instructions for Fabric Mats

Fabric Strips - Rip, rotary cut or cut poly/cotton or 100% cotton fabric into 44" x 2" wide strips.

Count Stitches - Each square on the pattern equals one stitch. Count squares on the chart. Count cross bars on the mat. Mats vary in size so it is important to count every mat you plan to use. Mark the center.

Center Design - Center the design on the mat before you begin to stitch.

Stitch Design - Work the design with giant Cross Stitches. Each stitch is made with a diagonal / and a return diagonal \ to form an X. Begin in the center and count each X.

Stitch the Background - Fill in the background with giant Cross Stitches. Knot ends of fabric on the backside of the mat.

Optional - Make giant White Stitches around the border of the mat.

Fabric Mats

As Americans began covering their floors with expensive hand-loomed carpets from the Orient, they needed a protective rug to guard against damaging sparks flying out of the fireplace, and to protect against muddy feet. Hence the origin of the small "hearth" or "welcome" rug.

Coincidentally, the hearth rug became a bright and ornamental addition to the hearthstone during warmer months when the fireplace was not in use. Collectors have found rugs featuring colorful floral designs and nautical images. Patriotic motifs were popular after the War of 1812.

With changes in lifestyle, small rugs are now used as welcome mats at the front door, as dirt deterrents by the back door, as foot savers in the kitchen, however, we still draw on the same folk art motifs and classic patriotic designs. These durable fabric mats can be used as decoration in almost every room of the home.

Today fabric mats are simple to make. By using an inexpensive grass mat as the base, a complete rug can be finished in just a few hours. The design colors can be customized to blend with any decor.

Turning old clothing and scraps of fabric into a useful item is always satisfying. I like to stitch a single small heart in the center of a mat to give as a housewarming gift... these little mats last for years.

Birdhouses in the Sky
Place a welcome mat on the back porch or in a sunroom, and a flock of neighbors will fly by for a bird's eye view.

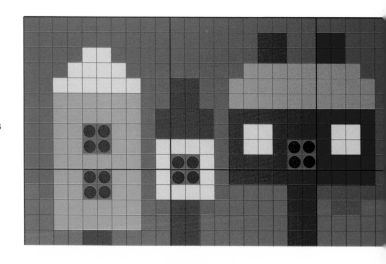

DESIGN SIZE: 25 holes wide x 15 holes high
FABRIC:

Design	Color	Number of Strips	Yards
House, Roof	Red Plaid	1	⅛
House, Roof, 2 Windows	Tan Print	5	½
Birdhouse, Roof, Poles	Brown Print	13	1
Windows, Doors	Black	3	¼
Grass	Green	9	¾
Background	Blue	17	1¼

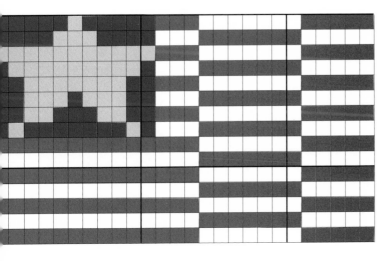

All American Red, White & Blue

An American flag welcomes
Fourth of July celebraters
to any summer picnic.

Flag Mat

DESIGN SIZE: 26 holes wide x 15 holes high
FABRIC:

Design	Color	Number of Strips	Yards
Star	Tan Print	6	½
Field	Dark Blue Print	9	¾
Stripes	Off White	24	1½
	Dark Red Print	28	1¾

Halloween Happy

When trick or treaters come for something good to eat, they'll be happy to see this friendly jack o' lantern under their feet.

DESIGN SIZE: 24 holes wide x 15 holes high
FABRIC:

Design		Color	Number of Strips	Yards
Background		Green	21	1½
Pumpkin		Dark Orange	24	1½
Face		Black	5	½
Grass, Leaf		Dark Green	13	1
Stem		Brown Print	1	⅛

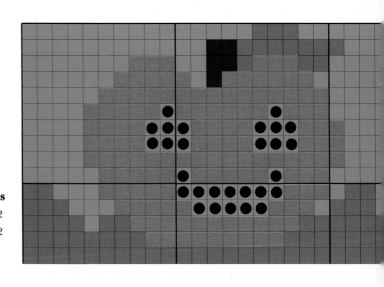

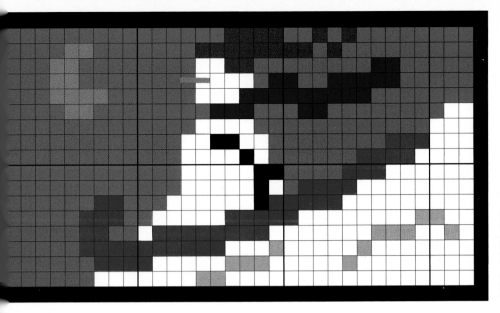

INSTRUCTIONS:
After mat is stitched, add nose, eye, mouth, buttons and scarf fringe with Black yarn or Black fabric strips.

...ledding Snowman Mat

...SIGN SIZE: 34 holes wide x 19 holes high
...BRIC:

...sign		Color	Number of Strips	Yards
...y		Blue Green	42	2¾
...owman, Hill		Ivory Print	29	2
...adows		Beige Print	3	¼
...on, Nose		Gold Print	4	¼
...t		Dark Blue Print	3	¼
...arf		Burgundy Print	4	¼
...d		Dark Red Print	10	¾
...m, Border		Black	12	¾

Snowy Sled Day

Remember the joys of childhood . . . the first snowfall, sledding to the bottom of the hill and mom saying "Don't forget your hat and scarf on this winter day!"

Mothers' hands have a way of weaving memories into everyday life. After baby's clothes are outgrown, the material is stitched into a heartwarming reminder of the first year.

Patchwork Hearts Mat

DESIGN SIZE: 43 holes wide x 24 holes high
FABRIC:

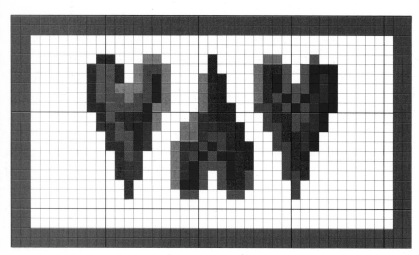

Design	Color	Number of Strips	Yards
Border, Red Patches	Dark Red Print	46	3
Background	Gold/Black Dot	62	4
Patches	Blue/Black Check	7	½
	Purple	6	½
	Burgundy Print	4	¼
	Burgundy	4	¼
	Mauve Print	7	½
	Teal	7	½
	Dark Teal	7	½
	Blue	6	½
	Red	6	½

Guardian Angel

"Good night, sleep tight, a guardian angel will watch over you until daylight."

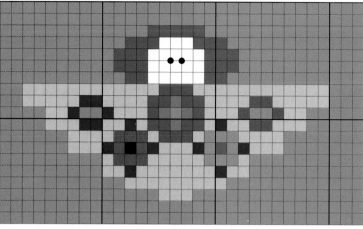

Flower Angel Mat

DESIGN SIZE: 33 holes wide x 19 holes high
FABRIC:

Design		Color	Number of Strips	Yards
Background		Blue Print	57	3⅝
Hair		Gold/Brown Print	5	½
Face		Ivory Print	3	¼
Wings		Tan Check	21	1½
Flowers		Burgundy Dot	3	¼
		Blue Print	1	⅛
		Dark Blue Print	1	⅛
		Dark Red	1	⅛
		Gold Print	1	⅛
		Dark Gold Print	2	⅛
		Mauve Print	1	⅛
		Brown	1	⅛
		Teal	1	⅛
		Dark Teal	1	⅛

INSTRUCTIONS:
After mat is finished, make eyes with Blue or Brown yarn.

Six Pretty Petals Mat

DESIGN SIZE: 35 holes wide x 20 holes high

FABRIC:

Design		Color	Number of Strips	Yards
Background		Green Check	50	3¼
Flower 1		Blue Check	10	¾
Center		Light Blue	2	⅛
Flower 2		Gold/Black Dot	10	¾
Center		Brown Print	2	⅛
Flower 3		Blue/Tan Check	10	¾
Center		Burgundy Dot	2	⅛
Flower 4		Dark Red	10	¾
Center		Tan/Blue Stripe	2	⅛
Flower 5		Teal	10	¾
Center		Beige Print	2	⅛
Flower 6		Gold Floral	11	¾
Center		Gold/Brown Print	2	⅛

INSTRUCTIONS:
After mat is finished, add cross stitch in center of each flower with Black yarn or Black fabric strips.

Pretty Flowers
With this pattern, stitch a bedside rag rug to match your favorite country quilt.

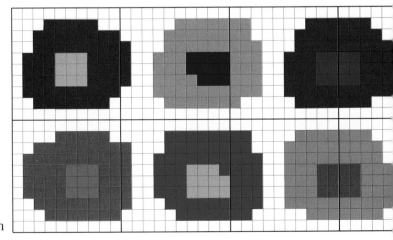

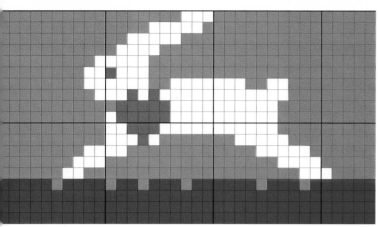

Rabbit Mat

DESIGN SIZE: 35 holes wide x 19 holes high
FABRIC:

Design	Color	Number of Strips	Yards
Background, Eye	Brown Print	55	3½
Rabbit	Beige Floral Print	22	1½
Grass	Green Check	20	1½
Heart	Red Dot	3	¼
Eye	Brown	1	⅛

Hoppin' a Long Bunny

Celebrate the blossoming of Spring with a welcoming white rabbit leaping into the season's first green grass.

Basic Instructions for Scrap Quilts

Cut Out - Trace patterns for applique motifs from the book. Iron fusible webbing onto the back of fabric pieces. Cut out motifs from fabrics. Cut two layers of cotton quilt batting for the background.

Stitch Patches - Stitch patch pieces together for borders and backgrounds.

Center Fabrics - Center backing and fabric background on two layers of cotton quilt batting. Pin or baste in place.

Position Pieces Position fabric motifs and pin in place.

Applique - Zig-Zag stitch designs in place with a sewing machine or hand-stitch designs in place.

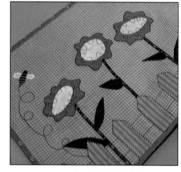

Add Binding - Pin and sew a strip of fabric binding around the front edge with right sides together. Turn binding under to the back (turn the edge under, miter the corners) then hand-stitch in place.

Scrap Quilts

For those who did not grow up making quilts at mother's side, the perfect stitch and design seems elusive. But the techniques are simple. Use a variety of fabric colors and prints. Cut applique designs free hand or from a pattern. Layer the cut-outs on base fabric. Then, stitch around the design to outline the image. The word "applique" simply means to apply cut pieces of one material to the surface of another.

Delicate, graceful and patterned, applique is constructed from small pieces of fabric that are often quite inexpensive. The method allows the most frugal use of fabric because out of only a small amount - 1/4 to 1/2 yard for example - can come all the applique motifs for a full quilt and the fabric can be cut to the best advantage without waste. In the 1800's, this was especially important in the case of scarce, expensive, often imported chintz. The method itself gave birth to the slang term "chintzy", meaning tight-fisted or cheap.

In accordance with the frugal nature of applique, most of my collection of fabric scraps comes from garage sales or tag sales as they are named on the East Coast. On Saturday mornings, my sister and I rise early to scout out the best sales. We want to be the first to arrive so that the best selection of fabrics is still available.

Some purchases we buy for pennies and for others we'll spend a dollar or two. Great finds are easy to spot and we've been known to come home with a carload of goodies. Although, I'll have to admit, we've become quite picky over the years and now search primarily for designer patterns and finer fabrics like silks, brocades and taffetas.

Flowers in the Garden Placemat

FABRIC: 14½" x 12" pieces of muslin and Tan check for front and back • 7" square of Red print for flowers • ¼" strips of Green print for stems • 6" square of Green for leaves • Seven 1¼" x 3½" strips of Tan/Red for fence • Scraps of Gold and White for bee • 1" strips of Gold print for binding • 6" square and 12" x 14½" piece of Warm & Natural batting

MATERIALS: Fusible web • Black permanent marker

INSTRUCTIONS:

Following the manufacturer's instructions, fuse the web to the back of the flower, stem, leaf, fence, bee fabrics and batting square. Trace the patterns on the fabrics and cut the flowers from Red print, the centers from batting and the leaves from Green fabric. Cut the stems from Green print strips. Referring to the photo, fuse the shapes on the front fabric. Machine

'Bee' Happy in the Garden

Classic quilts provide protection against the chill and add beauty to any room in your home.

applique and sew the spiral line for the bee, straight lines for the fence and curved lines on the flower centers. Draw the details on the bee with the marker. Stack the back, batting and front, pin together. Sew the binding to the long edges. Then sew the binding to the short edges turning the ends under.

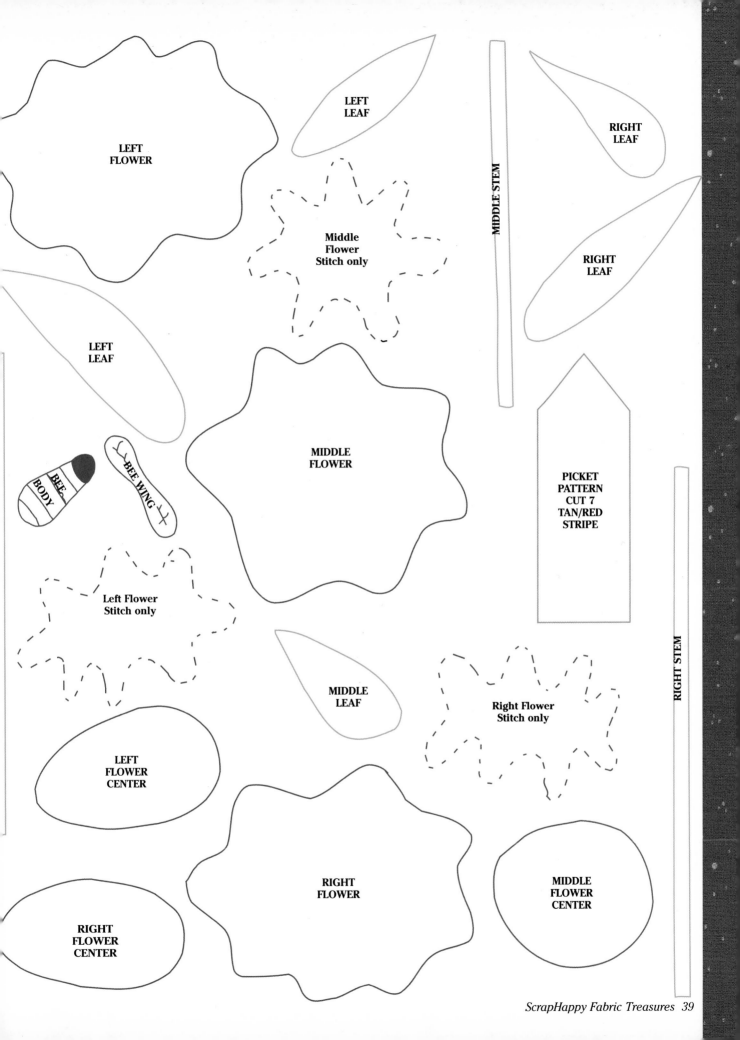

LEFT
FLOWER

LEFT
LEAF

RIGHT
LEAF

MIDDLE STEM

Middle
Flower
Stitch only

RIGHT
LEAF

LEFT
LEAF

MIDDLE
FLOWER

BEE
BODY

BEE WING

PICKET
PATTERN
CUT 7
TAN/RED
STRIPE

RIGHT STEM

Left Flower
Stitch only

MIDDLE
LEAF

Right Flower
Stitch only

LEFT
FLOWER
CENTER

RIGHT
FLOWER

MIDDLE
FLOWER
CENTER

RIGHT
FLOWER
CENTER

Snowman Placemat

FABRIC: $16\frac{1}{2}$" x 12" piece of Tan flannel for back • $3\frac{1}{2}$" x $16\frac{1}{2}$" piece of Tan/Green check flannel • 4" x $16\frac{1}{2}$" piece of Green/Black plaid • 6" x $16\frac{1}{2}$" piece of Green/Black stripe • Scraps of 3 coordinating prints • 1" strips of Black/Tan stripe for binding • 5" x 8" and 12" x $16\frac{1}{2}$" pieces of Warm & Natural batting

MATERIALS: Black and Gold embroidery floss • Spray bottle • Tea dye • Fusible web

INSTRUCTIONS:

Spray tea dye on a small piece of the batting, let dry. Following the manufacturer's instructions, fuse web to the back of the fabric scraps and the small piece of batting. Trace the snowman pattern on the batting and the stars on the scraps. Cut out the shapes. Transfer the embroidery pattern to the snowman.

Snowman - French knot the eyes and the mouth Black and straight stitch the nose Gold. Make 3 Black cross stitches for the buttons.

Placemat - Sew the $16\frac{1}{2}$" fabric pieces together for the front. Fuse the shapes in place and machine applique. Stack the flannel back, $16\frac{1}{2}$" batting and front, pin together. Sew the binding to the long edges. Then sew the binding to the short edges turning the ends under.

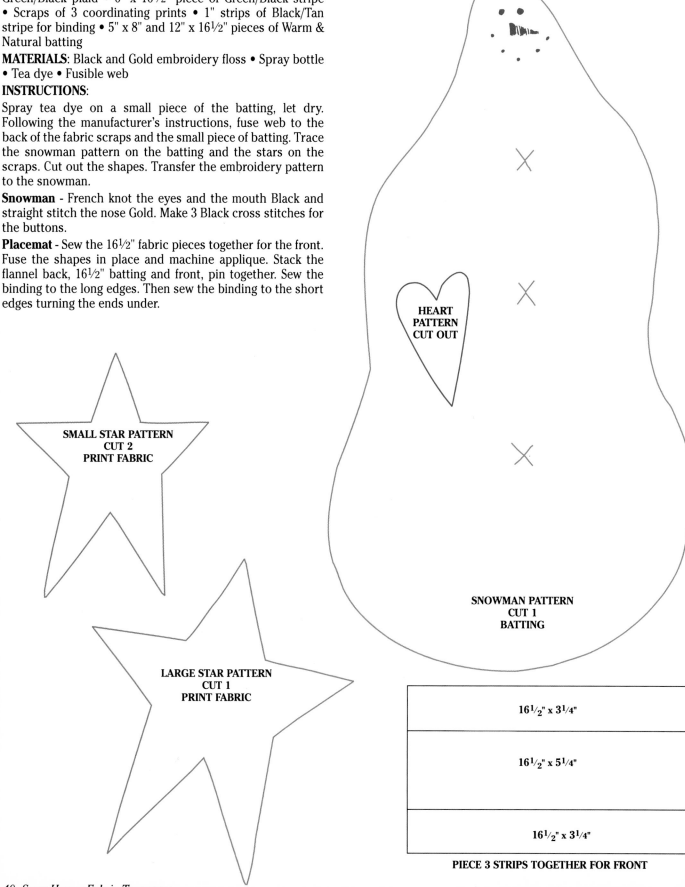

HEART PATTERN CUT OUT

SMALL STAR PATTERN
CUT 2
PRINT FABRIC

LARGE STAR PATTERN
CUT 1
PRINT FABRIC

SNOWMAN PATTERN
CUT 1
BATTING

| $16\frac{1}{2}$" x $3\frac{1}{4}$" |
| $16\frac{1}{2}$" x $5\frac{1}{4}$" |
| $16\frac{1}{2}$" x $3\frac{1}{4}$" |

PIECE 3 STRIPS TOGETHER FOR FRONT

Snowman Placemat Quilt

Folk art motifs are often cut free hand
like these stars. Even their floating
placement and multiple layered plaid fabric
resembles traditional folk art style.

Trick or Treat Wall Hanging

FABRIC: 13" x 14½" piece of Black for back • 2½" strips of 12 coordinating prints • Four 1" strips of muslin for center border • 8" x 10" piece and 1" strips of Black print for center and binding • 6" x 9" piece of Orange print for pumpkin • Scraps of Black for face and spider • Scrap of Green print for stem • Scrap of muslin for button • Warm & Natural batting

MATERIALS: 1¼" button cover kit • Four 1" buttons • Fine Gold thread • Black embroidery floss • Fusible web • Two ½" plastic rings for hanging • Black permanent marker

INSTRUCTIONS:

Wall Hanging - Trace the patterns. Following the diagram, cut 2½" strips to size. Assemble the patchwork using ¼" seam allowances. Following the manufacturer's instructions, fuse the web to the back of the hearts, pumpkin, face and stem fabrics. Transfer the patterns to the paper backing, cut out and fuse the shapes on the patchwork. Write 'Trick or Treat' around the center border with the marker. Stack the back, batting and patchwork pieces, pin together. Sew the binding to the short edges. Then sew the binding to the long edges turning the ends under.

Spider - Cut muslin to cover the button. Cut a ⁵⁄₈" Black circle, fuse on the center of the muslin. Back stitch the legs Black. Cover the button with the embroidered muslin following the kit instructions. Machine stitch the Gold spider web and sew the spider in place.

Finish - Sew the buttons on the corners and the plastic rings to the upper back corners.

BORDER HEART PATTERN

TRICK OR TREAT LARGE HEART PUMPKIN PATTERN

Happy Day

Just like a traditional quilt, the rectangle border and hearts could have been pieced together from scraps of fabric taken from worn clothing.

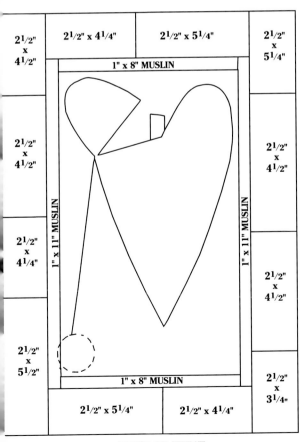

| 2¹⁄₂" x 4¹⁄₂" | 2¹⁄₂" x 4¹⁄₄" | 2¹⁄₂" x 5¹⁄₄" | 2¹⁄₂" x 5¹⁄₄" |

1" x 8" MUSLIN

2¹⁄₂" x 4¹⁄₂"

1" x 11" MUSLIN

2¹⁄₂" x 4¹⁄₂"

2¹⁄₂" x 4¹⁄₄"

1" x 11" MUSLIN

2¹⁄₂" x 4¹⁄₂"

2¹⁄₂" x 5¹⁄₂"

1" x 8" MUSLIN

2¹⁄₂" x 3¹⁄₄"

2¹⁄₂" x 5¹⁄₄"   2¹⁄₂" x 4¹⁄₄"

TRICK OR TREAT ASSEMBLY DIAGRAM

SPIDER PATTERN

SPIDER BACKGROUND PATTERN

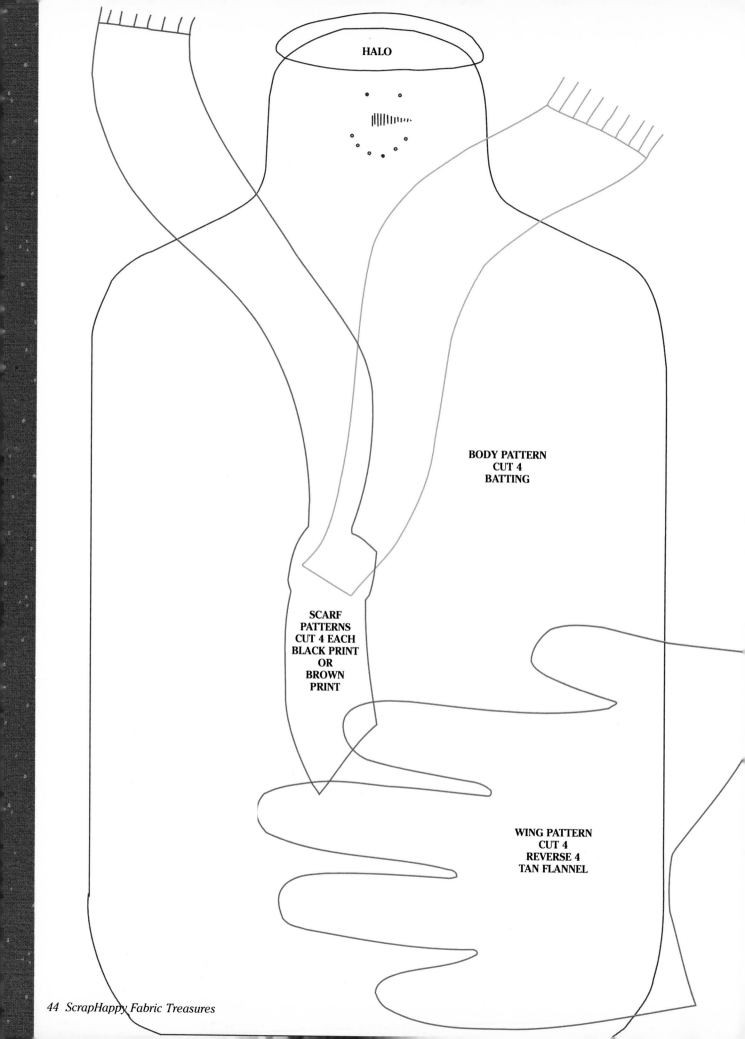

HALO

BODY PATTERN
CUT 4
BATTING

SCARF
PATTERNS
CUT 4 EACH
BLACK PRINT
OR
BROWN
PRINT

WING PATTERN
CUT 4
REVERSE 4
TAN FLANNEL

Snow Angels Gather Quilt

FABRIC: 29" square of muslin for back • Four 1½" x 29" Blue/Red plaid strips for border • Four 1½" x 29" Black/Tan plaid strips for binding • 14" squares of Blue, Red, Green and Brown prints for squares • ¼ yard of Tan flannel for wings • Four 6" x 8" pieces of Black or Brown print for scarves • 29" square and ½ yard of Warm & Natural batting for quilt and snow angels

MATERIALS: Twelve 1" buttons • Gold and Black embroidery floss • Fine Gold thread • Black permanent marker • Fusible web • Black sewing thread • Spray bottle of tea dye • Small sponge

INSTRUCTIONS:

Squares - Trace the patterns. Spray Tea dye on the batting for the snow angels, let dry. Following the manufacturer's instructions, fuse the web on the snow angels, wings and scarf fabrics. Transfer the patterns to the paper backing and cut out. Fold the squares diagonally, iron and unfold. Center the snow angels on the folds with the top of the heads 5" from corners. Place the wings under the angels and the scarves on the necks, fuse in place. Machine applique around the pieces with the Black

Angels of Snow

Unique design highlights these angels. The wings form a circular wreath and the flowing scarves almost put them in angelic motion.

thread. Embroider the noses Gold and dot the eyes and mouths with the marker. Machine stitch the halos with the Gold thread. Sew the buttons in place.

Quilt - Sew the squares together using ¼" seam allowances. Sew the 2 border strips to opposite sides of the quilt. Sew the border strips to the remaining edges overlapping the first strips. Stack the back, batting and front, pin together. Sew the binding to 2 opposite edges. Then sew the binding to the remaining edges, turning the ends under.

See snow Angel Doll instructions on page 66-67

Basic Instructions for Dolls

Transfer Patterns - Fold fabric with right sides together. Trace the pattern, transfer to cardboard and cut out. Place pattern on fabric then trace around pattern with a disappearing pen.

Stitch Layers - Machine stitch along the traced lines, stitching through two layers of fabric. Leave openings unstitched.

Cut Out Dolls - Cut out shapes 1/4" from the stitched lines. Clip curves and trim corners.

Turn and Stuff - Turn right side out through the openings. (If no openings are indicated, cut a slit in one layer of the fabric and turn right side out through the slit.) Stuff dolls with fiberfill. Sew openings closed. Sew arms and legs onto the body.

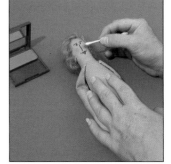

Embroider Details - Embroider facial features with 3-ply floss. Rub cheeks with Rose cosmetic 'blush' using a swab. Add details with floss, buttons, fabric yo-yos or beads.

Dress & Accessories - Trace blouse pattern and sew along line. Cut out 1/4" from stitched lines. Cut skirt to the size indicated then sew seams using a 1/4" seam allowance. Dress the doll.

Tea Dye: Mix two tablespoons of instant tea in a cup of hot water. Pour mixture into a spray bottle. Spray tea dye on fabrics. Hang to dry. Do not dry outside.

Heritage Dolls

In Colonial America, children played with simple dolls made from rags, feed sacks, leather, wood or corn husks. Only a fortunate child could own a fancy-dressed doll made from clothing. Fancy dolls were often adorned with ribbon, lace, charms, buttons and beads.

Today it is these trinkets and adornments which are our links to the past. Charms, buttons and beads have withstood time. They have been clipped from old clothing and saved as a reminder of the past. When you search through old boxes and drawers, look for these symbolic treasures to use as a link to your past. Adorn a doll, a quilt or any handmade item and turn it into a keepsake.

Several years ago, my sister, Brendy, came across a beautiful old quilt. At first sight she fell in love with its past, present and future. It had all the original stitching, handmade cottons and stuffing with a few cotton seeds left behind. But, over the years it had been badly stained and had acquired a notable burn hole.

Brendy's creative juices flowed into ideas of the holiday season and the future of that quilt changed forever. That Christmas, everyone in our family received a perfectly charming collection of quilted bears and little quilted heart ornaments made from that very quilt.

I treasure handmade keepsakes. The pieces of that quilt are one of my favorite pieces of history.

BODY PATTERN
CUT 2
TAN FLANNEL
(Leave bottom open)

LEAF
PATTERN
CUT 16
GREEN
PRINT

SHOE LACING
DIAGRAM

back of the head where knots will be covered by the hair, French knot eyes and straight stitch nose with the Tan floss and running stitch mouth with the Red floss. Glue the hair on the head, rub blush on the cheeks. Using the Red floss, sew 6 beads on each shoe crisscrossing between the beads. Tie the ends in a bow.

Dress - Trace the blouse pattern on the Tan flannel, cut out. With the wrong sides together, fold the strips for the bottom of the skirt in half, iron. With right sides together, sew the strips to the bottoms of the skirt pieces. Sew the skirt side seams and gather the top. Sew the shoulder and side seams of the blouse. Adjust the skirt to fit the blouse, sew together. Fold the sleeve ends under 1½", gather 1" from the edge with the Red floss. Put the dress on the doll. Pull the threads in the ends of the sleeves, adjust the gathers and tie a bow. Glue one button on the neck of the dress.

Wings - Place a layer of batting under a double layer of the Tan flannel. Trace the pattern, sew around the wings and cut out. Turn right side out, sew the opening closed and iron. Following the manufacturer's instructions, fuse the web to the wrong side of the Green print fabric. Transfer the vine and leaf patterns, cut out. Fuse the vine and leaves on the wings. Make the yo-yos. Glue the yo-yos on the wings and sew the buttons in place. Gather the center of the wings with floss, glue the wings on the doll.

Optional: Stiffen the wings with fabric stiffener on the back.

Merry Holidays Maiden Doll

FABRIC: Four 4" x 12" pieces of Tan flannel for blouse and wings • ¼ yard of Tan flannel for body • Two 6" x 8" pieces and six 2" circles of Red flannel star print for skirt and yo-yos • Two 1½" x 8" strips of Red/Tan stripe flannel for bottom of skirt • Scrap of Green print • 4" x 12" piece of batting

MATERIALS: 7 Brown buttons • 12 Brown seed beads • Tan and Red embroidery floss • Curly Red doll hair • Fusible web • Polyester fiberfill • Cosmetic blush • Cotton swab

INSTRUCTIONS:

Trace the patterns, transfer to the cardboard and cut out.

Body - Trace the body patterns on a double layer of flannel with right sides together. Sew leaving openings. Cut out, clip the curves and turn right side out. Stuff and hand stitch the openings closed. Sew the legs and arms on the body. Starting on the

Place on fold

Leave open

BLOUSE PATTERN
CUT 2
TAN FLANNEL

Leave open

Holly Days

Roses, berries and holly have long been favorite adornments for quilters. This pretty red skirted angel doll is surrounded by crimson petals and evergreen leaves.

ARM
PATTERN
CUT 4
TAN
FLANNEL

WING PATTERN
CUT 2
TAN FLANNEL
CUT
BATTING

SLEEVE

LEG PATTERN
CUT 4
TAN FLANNEL

YO-YO PATTERN
CUT 6
RED FLANNEL

To make yo-yo, fold edge under 1/8", sew with running stitch and pull stitches tight to gather. Tie off.

STEM PATTERNS
CUT 1 EACH
GREEN PRINT

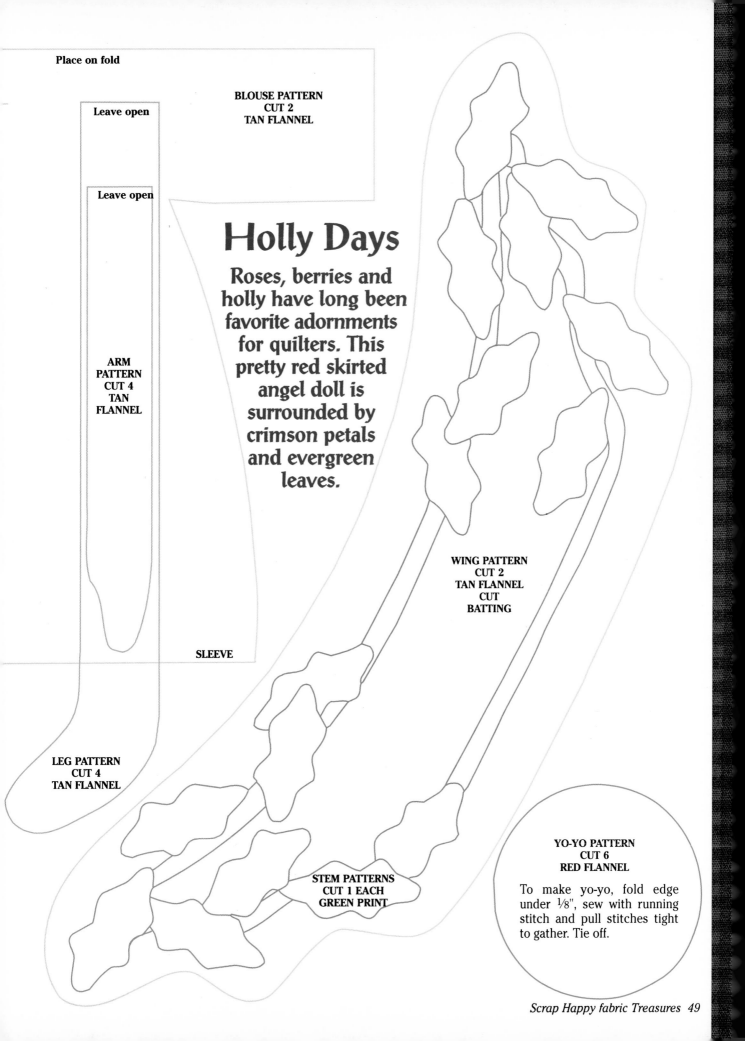

Patchwork Angel

FABRIC: Fourteen 1½" strips of assorted prints for body front and arms • 3" x 8½" piece of Black print for center front • 7" x 12" and 6" square of Tan/Black stripe for body back and legs • ½ yard of muslin for hands, head and wings

MATERIALS: Scrap of Brown paper for stars • Five ⅝" buttons • Black doll hair • Acrylic paint (Black, White, Flesh, Blue, Red, Brown, Metallic Gold) • White thread • Cosmetic blush • cotton swab

INSTRUCTIONS:

Trace the patterns, transfer to cardboard and cut out.

Body Front - To make the crazy quilt, sew the fabric together referring to the diagram.

Body - Cut a 1½" strip of the muslin. Sew the muslin and fabric strips together to make the arm fabric. Using double layers of fabric, trace the arm pattern on patchwork fabric, the legs on stripe fabric and the head on muslin. Stitch along the traced lines, cut out and turn right side out. Stuff the head. Stuff the arms leaving 6" in center unstuffed. Stuff 5" of the legs. Sew the legs to the center bottom of the body front. Stack the front and back body pieces with right sides together. Sew the shoulder seams leaving a 2" opening for the head. Sew the side and bottom seams. Turn right side out and stuff firmly. Paint the head Flesh. Insert and sew the head in the top opening.

Face - Paint the eyes White with large Blue and small Black dots and the mouth Red. Outline the eyes, nose and mouth Brown. Rub blush on the cheeks. Glue the hair on the head. Glue 3 buttons on the neck.

Arms - Sew the arms on the body at the shoulders bringing the White thread through the buttons and tying bows. Overlap the hands and glue.

Shoes - Paint the shoes Black. Paint the Brown paper Metallic Gold, cut out 2 stars and glue on the shoes.

Wings - Place a layer of the batting under a double layer of the muslin. Trace the pattern, sew around the wings and cut out. Turn right side out, sew the opening closed and iron. Machine stitch the design. Paint the wings Metallic Gold. Thin Black paint and outline the stitching. Glue the wings on the back.

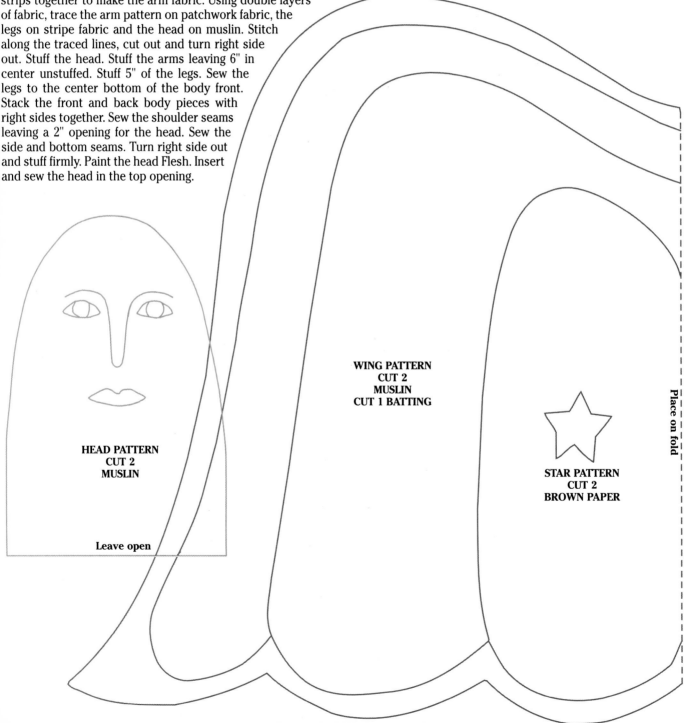

**HEAD PATTERN
CUT 2
MUSLIN**

Leave open

**WING PATTERN
CUT 2
MUSLIN
CUT 1 BATTING**

**STAR PATTERN
CUT 2
BROWN PAPER**

Place on fold

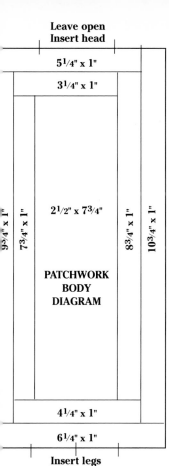

Leave open
Insert head

5¼" x 1"

3¼" x 1"

9¾" x 1" 7¾" x 1" 2½" x 7¾" 8¾" x 1" 10¾" x 1"

PATCHWORK
BODY
DIAGRAM

4¼" x 1"

6¼" x 1"

Insert legs

Leave open

LEG PATTERN
CUT 4
TAN/BLACK STRIPE

HAND PATTERN
CUT 4
MUSLIN

Leave open

PATCHWORK ARM DIAGRAM

2½" x 2½"   18½" x 2½"   2½" x 2½"

Log cabin style quilting
strips are form fitted
to the golden winged
angel pillow.

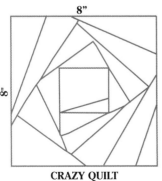

8"

8"

**CRAZY QUILT
DIAGRAM**

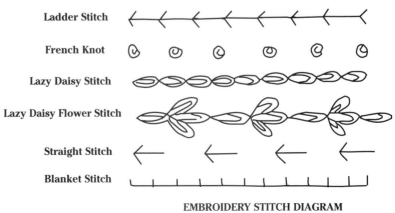

Ladder Stitch	
French Knot	
Lazy Daisy Stitch	
Lazy Daisy Flower Stitch	
Straight Stitch	
Blanket Stitch	

EMBROIDERY STITCH DIAGRAM

Brittany with Patchwork

FLANNEL: ½ yard of Tan for body back, arms, legs, head and quilt base • ¼ yard of Navy Blue for sleeves • ⅓ yard of Tan/Blue stripe for skirt • Scraps of coordinating Green, Red and floral print for patchwork

MATERIALS: Yarn hair • 6" of 2" Ecru lace • 20 assorted buttons • Off White and Green perle cotton • Brown and Red embroidery floss • Silk embroidery ribbon (Tan, Rose, Green, Blue, Gold) • Polyester fiberfill • 6" piece of cardboard • Cosmetic blush • cotton swab

INSTRUCTIONS: Trace patterns.

Body Front - To make the crazy quilt, cut an 8" square of the flannel for the base. Cut a 4" square of the Tan flannel and pin to the center of the base. Cut the scraps into 2" strips. To start, place a strip on one corner of the Tan square at an angle, sew with right sides together and trim off the excess fabric. Moving the base clockwise, continue sewing and trimming the strips as shown in the diagram. Embroider the sunflower using the Gold ribbon and straight stitches. French knot the center with the Brown floss. Make a series of lazy daisy stitches along 2 seams using the Blue and Tan ribbon. Make the lazy daisy flowers using the Rose and Green ribbon. Using the perle cotton, straight stitch one seam Off White, straight stitch one seam Green and blanket stitch one seam Off White.

Body - Sew a 3½" x 8" piece of the Tan flannel to the bottom of the crazy quilt for body front. Trace the arm, leg and head patterns on a double layer of the Tan flannel. Stitch along the traced lines, cut out and turn right side out. Stuff the head and 4" of the arms and legs. Cut four 3½" x 10½" pieces of the Navy Blue flannel for the sleeves. Stack one sleeve piece and one arm on each side of the body front, sew in place. Cut an 8" x 12" piece of the Tan flannel for the body back. Sew the remaining sleeve pieces on the back. Sew the legs to the center bottom of the body front. Stack the front and back body pieces with right sides together. Sew the shoulder seams leaving a 2" opening for the head. Sew the underarm sleeve seams. Sew the side and bottom seams stopping at the bottom of the sleeves and leaving 3" open on the bottom for turning. Stuff and sew the bottom opening closed. Insert and sew the head in the top opening.

Head - Make French knot eyes and straight stitch nose using the Brown floss and back stitch mouth using the Red floss. Rub blush on the cheeks. Wrap yarn around 6" piece of cardboard 20 times and tie in the center with a piece of the yarn. Cut along one edge of the cardboard and fray the ends. Glue the hair on the head. Wrap the yarn around 3 fingers 10 times for the bangs. Tie a knot in the center with a piece of yarn and cut along one edge. Glue in place.

Collar - Wrap the lace around the neck, overlap the ends matching motifs and glue.

Skirt - Cut a 12" x 44" piece of the stripe flannel. Sew the back seam and make a narrow hem at the bottom. Fold the top down 1", hand gather the top with the Off White perle cotton adding a button on every third stitch. Tie around the waist.

Finish - Turn the ends of the sleeves under 1½", hand gather 1" from the end using the Off White perle cotton, adjust the gathers and tie a bow. Glue 2 buttons on each foot.

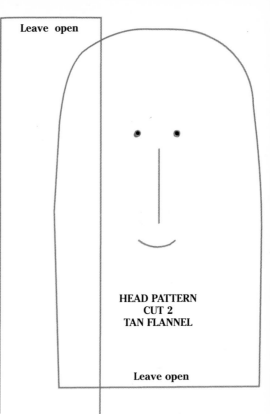

ARM PATTERN CUT 4 TAN FLANNEL

Leave open

HEAD PATTERN CUT 2 TAN FLANNEL

Leave open

LEG PATTERN CUT 4 TAN FLANNEL

SUNFLOWER DIAGRAM

Patches

Sunflower Sue makes you fall in love with scraps again. Fine triangles are organized in a simple pattern while stitching elegantly frames each patch piece.

Place on fold

Yolanda the Yo-Yo Lady Doll

DRESS
PATTERN
CUT 2
TAN FLANNEL

FABRIC: 1/3 yard of muslin for arms, legs and body • Two 11" x 23" pieces of Red check for skirt • Two 8" x 20" pieces of Tan flannel for blouse • Six 3¼" circles and twelve 3¼" x 5" print ovals for yo-yos • Two 6" x 16" pieces of Dark Red felt

MATERIALS: 6" x 16" piece of cardboard • Three ¾" and two ½" buttons • Polyester fiberfill • 2" grapevine wreath • Tiny Red berries • Blonde doll hair • Embroidery floss (Brown, Black, Red) • Cosmetic blush • cotton swab

INSTRUCTIONS:

Trace the patterns, transfer to the cardboard and cut out.

Body - Trace the body patterns on a double layer of the muslin. Sew, leave openings. Cut out, clip the curves and turn right side out. Stuff and hand stitch the openings closed. Sew the legs and arms on the body. Starting on the back of the head where the knots will be covered by the hair, French knot eyes and straight stitch the nose with Brown floss and straight stitch the mouth with Red floss. Glue the hair on the head, rub blush on the cheeks.

Dress - Trace the blouse pattern on the Tan flannel, cut out. Sew the skirt side seams and gather the top. Sew the shoulder and side seams of the blouse. Sew the ¾" buttons on the front. Adjust the skirt to fit the blouse, sew together. Fold the sleeve ends under 1½", gather 1" from the edge with Brown floss. Place the dress on the doll. Pull the threads in ends of the sleeves, adjust the gathers and tie a knot.

Wings - Trace the patterns and cut out one cardboard and 2 felt wings. Stack felt, cardboard and felt wings. Machine stitch ¼" from the edge. Make the yo-yos and glue on the front of the wings. Glue the wings on the back of the angel.

Finish - Glue the berries on the wreath and the wreath on the head. Glue the buttons on the feet.

BODY PATTERN
CUT 2
MUSLIN

WING PATTERN
CUT 2
DARK RED FELT
CUT 1 ON INNER LINE
CARDBOARD

YO-YO
PLACEMENT
DIAGRAM

Place on fold

OVAL YO-YO
PATTERN
CUT 12
PRINT FABRIC

ROUND YO-YO PATTERN
CUT 6
PRINT FABRIC

To make yo-yo, fold edge under ⅛", sew with running stitch and pull stitches tight to gather. Tie off.

Leave open

Yo-Yo Princess

All it takes is a stitch, a pull and a tuck, to make the pretty yo-yos on this doll's wings.

ARM PATTERN
CUT 4
MUSLIN

LEG PATTERN
CUT 4
MUSLIN

Place on fold

Leave open

BLOUSE PATTERN
CUT 2
TAN
FLANNEL

BUTTON ME UP ANGE
WING PATTERN
CUT 2
FELT

BODY PATTERN
CUT 2 MUSLIN

BUTTON ME UP
ANGEL
CARDBOARD
WING PATTERN
CUT 1

Button Me Up

FABRIC: $1/3$ yard of muslin for arms, legs and body • 11" x 32" piece of floral print flannel for skirt • $2^{1}/_{2}$" x 32" strip of Tan flannel for bottom of skirt • Two 7" x 21" pieces of Tan flannel for blouse • Two 7" x $18^{1}/_{2}$" pieces of Dark Green felt for wings

MATERIALS: 7" x $18^{1}/_{2}$" piece of cardboard • Assorted buttons to cover wings and for blouse • 8 Brown seed beads • Embroidery floss (Tan, Light Blue, Red, Green) • $1^{1}/_{2}$ yards of $1/4$" Gold ribbon • Blonde yarn doll hair • Flesh and Brown acrylic paint • Polyester fiberfill • Cosmetic blush • cotton swab

INSTRUCTIONS:

Trace the patterns, transfer to the cardboard and cut out.

Body - Trace the body patterns on a double layer of the muslin. Sew leaving openings. Cut out, clip the curves and turn right side out. Stuff and hand stitch the openings closed. Sew the legs and arms on the body. Paint the head, hands and legs Flesh. Paint the shoes Brown. Starting on the back of the head where the knots will be covered by the hair, French knot the eyes Blue, back stitch the nose and eyebrows Tan and straight stitch the mouth Red. Cut 14" pieces of the hair, tie in the center with a piece of hair and glue the center on the head. Tie into a pony tail with a $1/2$" x 8" piece of Green felt. Blush the cheeks. Glue 4 beads on each shoe.

Dress - Trace the blouse pattern on the Tan flannel, cut out. With wrong sides together, fold the strip for the bottom of the skirt in half, iron. With right sides together, sew the strip to the bottom of the skirt. Sew the skirt back seam and gather the top. Sew the shoulder and side seams of the blouse. Adjust the skirt to fit the blouse, sew together. Fold the sleeve ends under $1^{1}/_{2}$", gather 1" from the edge with the Green floss. Put the dress on the doll. Pull the threads in the ends of the sleeves, adjust the gathers and tie a bow. Glue one button on the neck of the dress.

Wings - Trace the patterns and cut out one cardboard and 2 felt wings. Stack felt, cardboard and felt wings. Machine stitch $1/4$" from the edge. Glue the buttons on the front of the wings. Tie the wings to the body crisscrossing the ribbon in the front and back and tying a bow at the waist.

Place on fold

Place on fold

Leave open

WING
ATTACHMENT
DIAGRAM

Place on fold

ave ends of
ms and legs
open

Button Collector
Collecting buttons can be useful to make an antique doll.

M PATTERN
CUT 4
MUSLIN

G PATTERN
CUT 4
MUSLIN

Authentic handmade dolls from the late 1800's started with home grown cotton. Women from colonial times filled their days hand-carding, home spinning, weaving and dyeing the fabric.

Adorable Bunny with Carrots

FABRIC: One yard of tea dyed muslin for heart, arms, legs, ears, body and skirt • 5½" x 24" piece of Blue stripe for blouse • 1¼" x 24" strip of Blue stripe for skirt bottom • Two ½" x 18" strips of Green print for bow

MATERIALS: Five ¾" buttons • White perle cotton • Acrylic paint (Tan, Burnt Orange, Terra Cotta) • Green permanent marker • 3" straw hat • Eucalyptus • Polyester fiberfill• Cosmetic blush • cotton swab

INSTRUCTIONS:

Trace the patterns, transfer to the cardboard and cut out.

Body - Trace the body patterns on a double layer of muslin. Sew leaving openings. Cut out, clip the curves and turn right side out. Stuff the body. Stuff the arms and legs leaving 3" at the top unstuffed. Hand stitch the openings closed. Sew the legs and arms on the body. Paint the head, hands, ears and legs Tan. Paint the center of ears, eyes, nose and cheeks Terra Cotta.

Dress - Trace the dress pattern on the stripe fabric, cut out. Cut two 12" x 17" pieces of the muslin for skirt. On skirt front trace carrot pattern with Green marker and paint carrot with Orange paint. Let dry. With wrong sides together, fold the strip for the bottom of the skirt in half, iron. With right sides together, sew the strip to the long edges of the skirt pieces. Sew the skirt side

seams and gather the top. Sew the shoulder and side seams of the dress top. Adjust the skirt to fit the dress top, sew together. Fold the sleeve ends under 1½", gather 1" from the edge with the perle cotton. Place the dress on the doll. Pull the threads ends of the sleeves, adjust the gathers and tie a bow. Glue 2 buttons on the front of the dress.

Heart - Fold the muslin with right sides together. Trace the heart pattern. The traced line is the sewing line. Sew along the traced line, cut out leaving a ¼" seam allowance, make slit in the back layer and turn right side out. Stuff the heart with fiberfill. Hand stitch the slit closed. Tie fabric strips around the heart. Sew perle cotton through the top of the heart, 2 buttons, hand and a button. Tie ends in a bow to secure.

Finish - Fold the tops of the ears and glue on the head. Glue the leaves around the crown of the hat, fold up the front and glue one leaf in the center front of the brim. Glue the hat on the head.

CARROT PATTERN

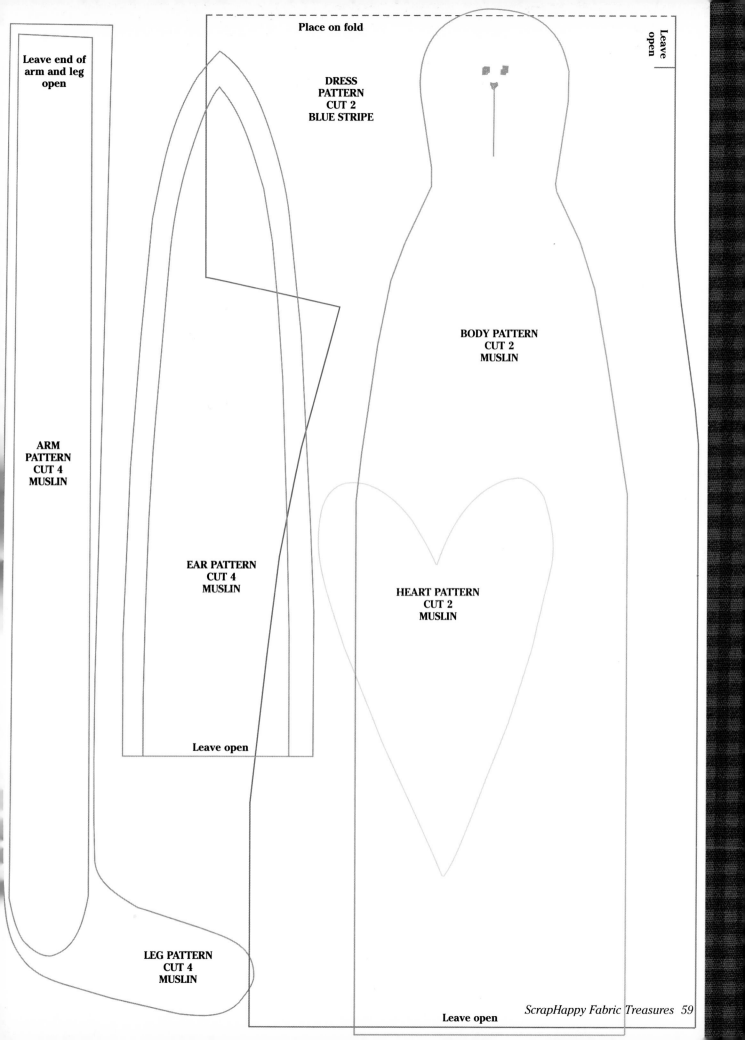

Leave end of arm and leg open

Place on fold

Leave open

DRESS PATTERN CUT 2 BLUE STRIPE

BODY PATTERN CUT 2 MUSLIN

ARM PATTERN CUT 4 MUSLIN

EAR PATTERN CUT 4 MUSLIN

HEART PATTERN CUT 2 MUSLIN

Leave open

LEG PATTERN CUT 4 MUSLIN

Leave open

Autumn Doll with Pumpkins

FABRIC: Two 4" x 9" pieces and two 8" x 10" pieces of Tan check for blouse and skirt • ¼ yard of muslin for doll body and scarecrow head • 18" x 23" piece of Gold tulle for underskirt • Four 4" squares of muslin for pumpkin • Fourteen 2½" circles of Green for yo-yos • 4" x 8" piece of Green for scarecrow dress • ½" x 8" strip of Green for scarecrow belt • ¼" x 5" strip of Black for hat • 60" x ½" torn strip of Black for leg stripes • 3½" circle of Black felt for scarecrow hat

MATERIALS: Polyester fiberfill • 4" thick and 3" thin cinnamon sticks • 2 Brown and 6 Black ⅝" buttons • Acrylic paint (Burnt Orange, Dark Green, Brown, Black, Red) • Black permanent marker • Brown raffia • 3" straw hat • Berry cluster • Cosmetic blush • cotton swab • Raffia

INSTRUCTIONS:

Trace the patterns, transfer to the cardboard and cut out.

Body - Trace the body patterns on a double layer of the muslin. Sew leaving openings. Cut out, clip the curves and turn right side out. Stuff and hand stitch the openings closed. Sew the legs and arms on the body. Paint the mouth Red and draw the eyes and nose with the marker. Rub blush on the cheeks. Glue raffia on the head for the hair.

Legs - Paint the shoes Black. Glue 6 strips of torn Black fabric around each leg at ¼" intervals. Glue a Black button on each shoe.

Dress - Trace the blouse pattern on the check fabric, cut out. Cut two 8" x 10" pieces of the check fabric for the skirt. Sew the skirt side seams on 8" edges and gather the top. Fold the sleeve ends under ¼" and hem. Sew the shoulder and side seams of the blouse. Adjust the skirt to fit the blouse, sew together. Put the dress on the doll. Glue 2 Brown buttons on the front of the dress. Fold the tulle in half lengthwise, gather one edge, place on the doll under the dress, pull the gathers tight and tie off. Make the yo-yos from the Green circles, glue on the dress hem.

Pumpkins - Fold the muslin with right sides together. Trace 2 pumpkin patterns on the muslin. The traced lines are the sewing lines. Sew along the traced lines, cut out leaving a ¼" seam allowance, make a slit in back layers and turn right side out. Stuff the pumpkins with fiberfill. Hand stitch the slits closed. Paint the pumpkins Burnt Orange with Green stems. Shade the lines Black. Sew 2 Black buttons on each pumpkin with the Black floss.

Scarecrow - Glue the center of the 3" cinnamon stick 1½" from top of the 4" cinnamon stick in a 't' shape. Cut the head from the muslin. Draw the face with the marker and rub blush on the cheeks. Place small ball of fiberfill in the center and hand gather ½" from the edge. Pull the gathers leaving a small opening. Glue the head on the top of the 4" cinnamon stick. Loosely gather the felt hat along stitching line with the Black floss. Glue the hat on the head. Cut 2 scarecrow dress pieces. Sew the side seams and cut down the center of the front. Place the dress on the scarecrow, tie the belt around the waist.

Finish - Glue the scarecrow hands on the pumpkins. Sew the pumpkins to the doll's hands. Glue a band around the hat, turn up the front and glue the berries in place. Glue the hat on the head.

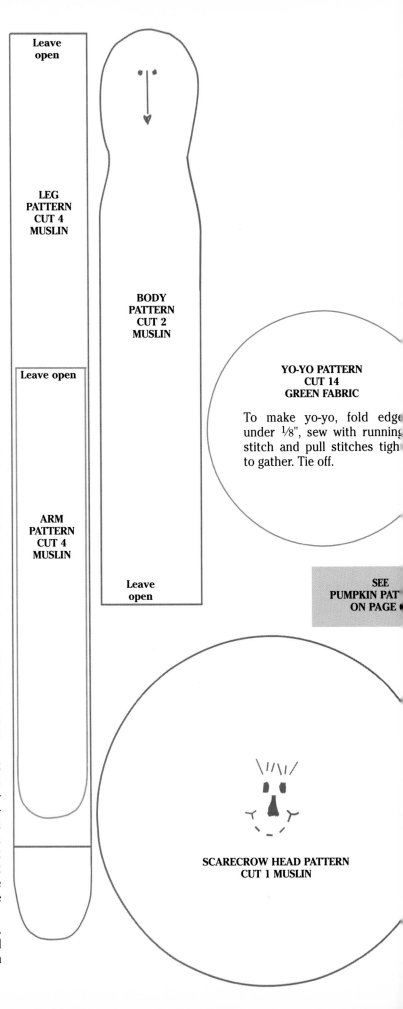

LEG PATTERN CUT 4 MUSLIN

Leave open

BODY PATTERN CUT 2 MUSLIN

Leave open

ARM PATTERN CUT 4 MUSLIN

Leave open

YO-YO PATTERN CUT 14 GREEN FABRIC

To make yo-yo, fold edge under ⅛", sew with running stitch and pull stitches tight to gather. Tie off.

SEE PUMPKIN PAT ON PAGE

SCARECROW HEAD PATTERN CUT 1 MUSLIN

Leave open

AUTUMN
BLOUSE PATTERN
CUT 2
TAN CHECK

Place on fold

Pumpkins

A harvest princess
holds prized pumpkins
and a scarecrow as signs of
the year's bountiful harvest.

Place on fold

SCARECROW
DRESS PATTERN
CUT 2
GREEN

Place on fold

SCARECROW
HAT PATTERN
CUT 1 ON FOLD
BLACK FELT

Stitching line

Octoberfest celebrates the season's fruits. Fair days sport contests for the largest pumpkin, sweetest corn and most accomplished needlework.

Pumpkin Gardener

FABRIC: Two 8" x 12" pieces of Black/Gold check flannel for dress and base • 4½" x 12" piece of muslin for apron • Two 3" squares of muslin for head

MATERIALS: 3" Black straw hat • 2" straw basket with handle • Embroidery floss (Dark Green, Orange, Black, Tan) • Three ⅝" buttons • Burnt Orange and Black acrylic paint • Polyester fiberfill • 9" of ¼" Tan ribbon • Two 4" twigs • Black curly doll hair • Green craft wire • Green sheet moss • 2 small nuts for pumpkins • Doll pellets

INSTRUCTIONS:

Trace the patterns, transfer to the cardboard and cut out.

Body - Trace the body pattern on a double layer and base on a single layer of the check flannel. Sew the side and underarm seams on the traced lines. Sew the base to the bottom. Sew the shoulder seams leaving opening for the head. Turn right side out. Place 1" layer of the pellets in the bottom of the body. Stuff the rest of the body with fiberfill.

Head - Trace the head pattern on the muslin, sew along the traced line, turn right side out and hand stitch along the bottom of the head. Stuff the head and pull the stitches to gather, tie off. Paint the head Burnt Orange and the face Black. Insert the head in the body opening and glue.

Arms - Insert the twigs in the sleeves, stuff with fiberfill leaving 1" unstuffed and tie the sleeves around the twigs with the Black floss.

Apron - Cut the pockets from scraps of the checked fabric straight stitch to the front of the apron with the Black floss. Back stitch the stem line and leaves Dark Green and French knot the flowers Orange. Hand gather the top of the apron with the Tan floss, tie around the waist with a bow in the back. Glue the sleeves to the sides of the body and the top of the apron.

Basket - Paint the nuts Burnt Orange and the faces Black. Fill the basket with moss and glue the nuts in the basket. Coil 2 pieces of the wire around a pencil and attach to the handle. Sew the basket to one sleeve.

Finish - Glue the buttons on the front of the body. Glue the hair on the head. Glue the ribbon around the hat and a button on the ribbon. Glue the hat on the head.

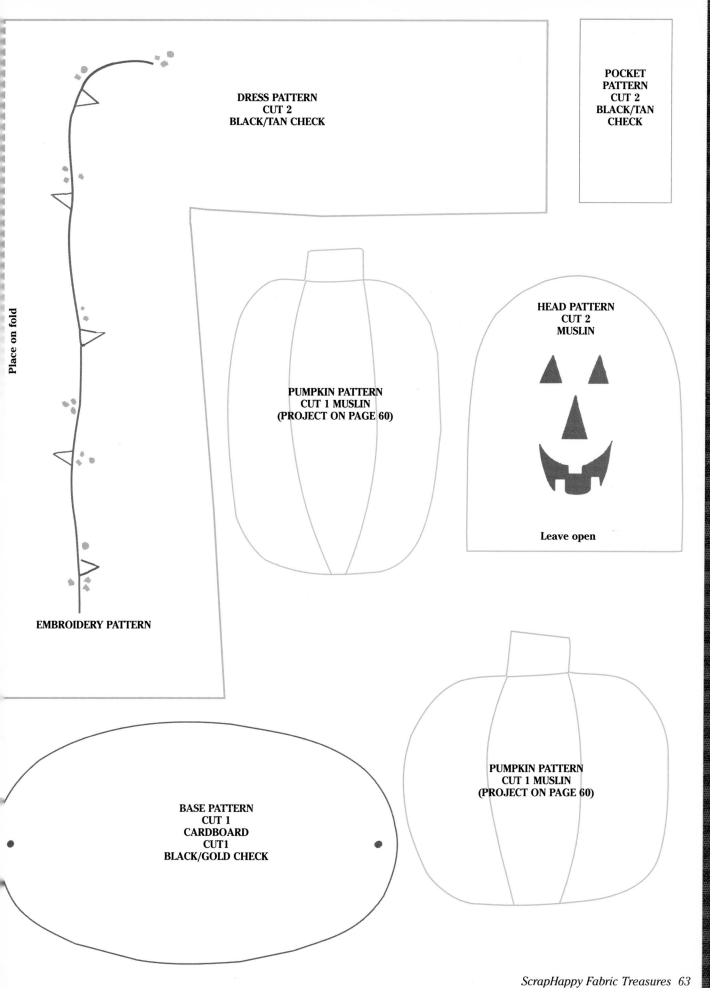

DRESS PATTERN
CUT 2
BLACK/TAN CHECK

POCKET
PATTERN
CUT 2
BLACK/TAN
CHECK

Place on fold

EMBROIDERY PATTERN

PUMPKIN PATTERN
CUT 1 MUSLIN
(PROJECT ON PAGE 60)

HEAD PATTERN
CUT 2
MUSLIN

Leave open

BASE PATTERN
CUT 1
CARDBOARD
CUT1
BLACK/GOLD CHECK

PUMPKIN PATTERN
CUT 1 MUSLIN
(PROJECT ON PAGE 60)

Wildflower

FABRIC: 8" square of muslin for head and arms • Two 4½" x 5½" pieces of Brown print for skirt • 5" square of Black stripe for legs • Two 5" x 8" pieces of Tan flannel for wings • ½" x 10" strip of Green check for bow

MATERIALS: Three ⅝" buttons • Three assorted shank buttons for flowers • 3 small twigs for stems • Polyester fiberfill • Acrylic paint (Flesh, Green, Tan, Red) • Black permanent marker • Blonde yarn hair

INSTRUCTIONS:

Trace the patterns, transfer to the cardboard and cut out.

Body - Trace the blouse and arms on the muslin, the skirt on the Brown print and the legs on the stripe fabrics. Sew the blouse pieces to the skirt pieces. Sew the head, arms and legs, turn right side out. Stuff the head, hands and all but the top 1" of the legs. Sew the arms and head on the blouse front and the legs on the skirt front. Sew the blouse/skirt pieces leaving an opening on the side of the skirt. Turn right side out, stuff and hand stitch the side opening closed. Glue the back blouse seam to the back of the head. For the hair, cut 2" pieces of yarn, tie in center with a piece of yarn and glue on the head. Ravel the yarn ends.

Paint - Paint the head and hands Flesh. Paint the mouth and cheeks Red. Outline the mouth and draw the eyes, eyebrows and nose with the marker. Paint the blouse Tan. Make Green dots and draw circles with the marker.

Wings - Fold the flannel with right sides together, trace the wing pattern, stitch along the traced lines and cut out leaving a ¼" seam allowance. Slit one layer and turn right side out. Sew the opening closed. Machine stitch around the wings ⅛" from the edge. Paint the back of the wings Tan to stiffen. Glue the wings on the back of the doll.

Finish - Glue the ⅝" buttons on the waist. For the flowers, glue the twigs in the holes of the shank buttons. Tie a Green fabric strip bow around the flowers, glue on the waist behind the hands.

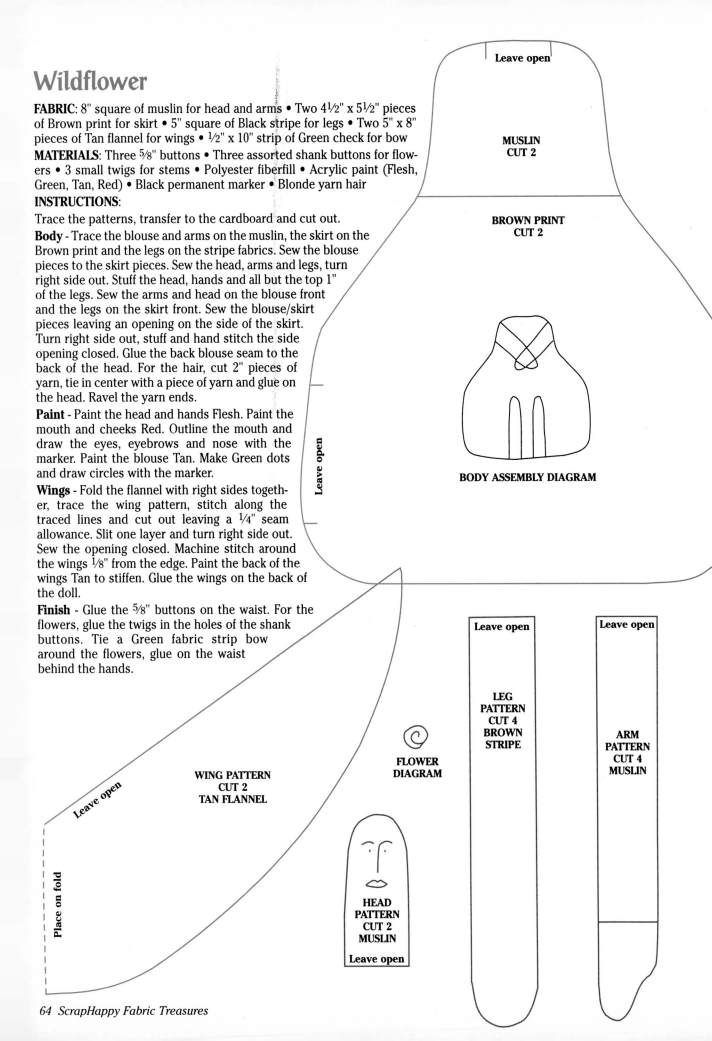

MUSLIN
CUT 2

BROWN PRINT
CUT 2

Leave open

BODY ASSEMBLY DIAGRAM

Leave open

WING PATTERN
CUT 2
TAN FLANNEL

Place on fold

FLOWER
DIAGRAM

LEG
PATTERN
CUT 4
BROWN
STRIPE

Leave open

ARM
PATTERN
CUT 4
MUSLIN

Leave open

HEAD
PATTERN
CUT 2
MUSLIN

Leave open

'Angelique'

Handmade dolls send special messages to family and friends.

Snowflake the Snow Angel

Recycled knit gloves form wings for this angelic snowman. A delicate navy floss stitched into snowflakes on the fingers is the perfect touch.

FABRIC: ½ yard of Warm & Natural batting for body• 3½" x 35" strip of Blue plaid fabric for scarf • Two 4" squares of Black felt for purse • 4" square of Tan flannel •

MATERIALS: Pair of cotton knit gloves • 4" grapevine wreath • Two 7" twigs • 7 peppercorns • Moss Green and Black embroidery floss • Oven bake clay • 3 large Black buttons • Burnt Orange acrylic paint • Polyester fiberfill • Spray bottle • Fabric stiffener • Tea dye • White glue • Gold glitter • Pinking shears

INSTRUCTIONS:

Body - Tea dye the batting, let dry. Trace the pattern, transfer to the cardboard and cut out. Trace the pattern on a double layer of the batting, sew on the traced line leaving the opening and turn right side out. Stuff with fiberfill and sew the opening closed. Water down glue, spread over the front of the body and sprinkle with the glitter, let dry. Sew the buttons on the front and knot the thread on the back of the body. Make the holes in the shoulders, insert and glue the twigs in place for arms.

Wings - Straight stitch the snowflakes on the gloves using the Black floss. Tea dye the gloves and let dry. Dip the gloves in fabric stiffener, lay flat and let dry. Glue the wings on the back of the body.

Face - Following the manufacturer's instructions, soften the clay and form a ¼" x 1¼" nose. Bake and cool. Paint nose Burnt Orange and glue on the face. Glue the peppercorns for mouth and eyes. Glue the wreath on the head and tie the scarf around the neck.

Purse - Trace the patterns. Cut heart from the flannel. Cut the purse from the felt using pinking shears. Straight stitch the snowflake on heart using the Black floss. Add French knots to the ends of the longest stitches. Sew the heart to one piece of the felt. Sew the purse front to the back leaving the top open. Cut three 19" pieces of Moss Green floss, braid and tie knots in the ends. Glue the ends to the front of the purse. Hang the purse over one shoulder.

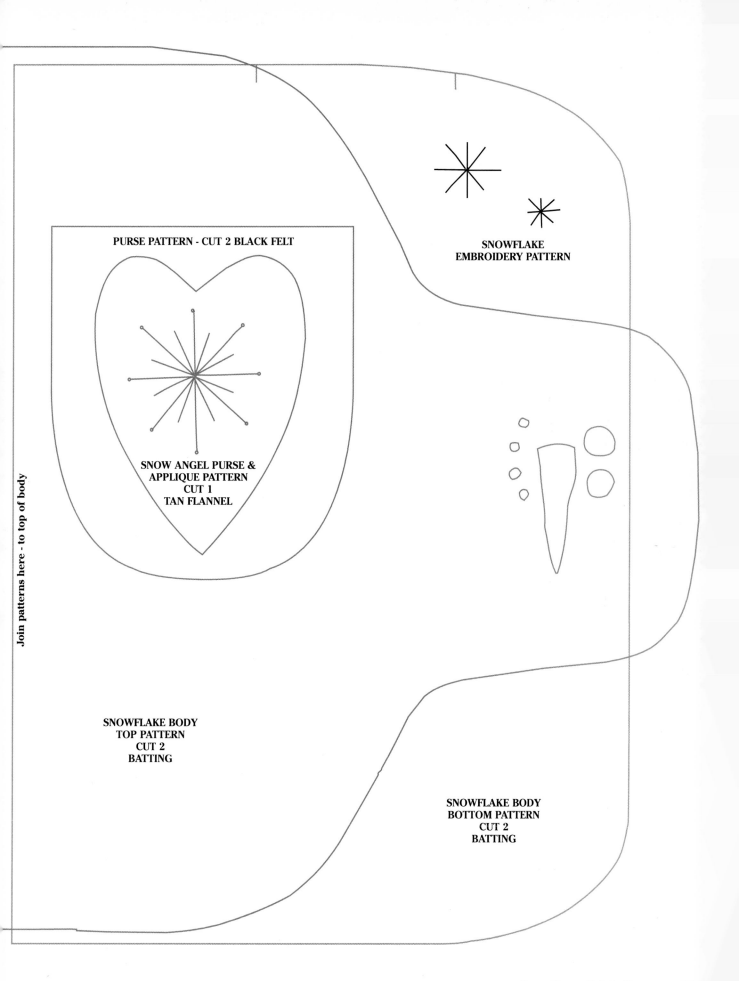

Join patterns here - to top of body

PURSE PATTERN - CUT 2 BLACK FELT

SNOW ANGEL PURSE &
APPLIQUE PATTERN
CUT 1
TAN FLANNEL

SNOWFLAKE
EMBROIDERY PATTERN

SNOWFLAKE BODY
TOP PATTERN
CUT 2
BATTING

SNOWFLAKE BODY
BOTTOM PATTERN
CUT 2
BATTING

Scarecrow   *by Rochelle Norris*

WOOD PARTS: Doll body • 5" piece of ¼" dowel • 3 bird cutouts • 3" sign

FABRIC: ¼ yard of leaf print for shirt • 7" x 17" piece of patchwork print for pants • 1" x 9" piece of patchwork print for straps

DECOART ACRYLIC PAINT: Raw Sienna • Black • Brandy Wine • Yellow Ochre

MATERIALS:

6" twig • Raffia • 4" clay pot • Florist tape • Florist foam • Spanish moss • 4" straw hat • Cosmetic blush • cotton swab • Identi Pen

INSTRUCTIONS:

Doll - Cut the doll piece from pine using the pattern on page 71. Wash the head lightly with Raw Sienna, shade Raw Sienna and

Grow where you're planted.

spatter Black. Rub the cheeks with blush and dot the eyes Black. Draw a smile with the Identi Pen. Paint the nose Brandy Wine. Drill ¼" holes for the arms and hole in bottom of the body. Glue the dowel in bottom of the body.

Arms - For each arm, cut forty 5" to 6" pieces of the raffia. Hold one end of the pieces together and wrap the ends with florist tape.

Shirt - Make the shirt. Fold bottom edges of the sleeves under 1¼". Hand stitch around the openings 1" from the folded edges. Glue the arms in the sleeves. Put the shirt on the doll, pull thread at the neck, adjust the gathers and tie a knot. Wrap 3 pieces of raffia around the neck, tie a bow.

Pants - With right sides together, sew the back seam of the pants (Dia. #1). Fold under the top and bottom edges ½" and hand stitch around the opening ⅛" from the folded edge (Dia #2)

Place the pants on the doll with the top at waist and bottom 3" from bottom of the dowel. Pull the thread, adjust the gathers and tie a knot. Tie a knot in one end of each strap. Glue the knots to the front of the pants. Drape the straps over the shoulders, cross in the back and glue the ends to the back of the pants, cut ends at an angle.

Sign - Paint the edges of the sign Raw Sienna brushing a little over the front edge. Write 'No Crows' and make the dots with an Identi pen. Glue a twig in the sign hole.

Crows - Paint the crows Black, detail Yellow Ochre.

Finish - Cut florist foam to fit inside the pot. Cover with moss. Glue and insert the dowel in the foam. Cut short pieces of raffia for the hair. Glue the hair and hat on the head. Glue and insert the sign in the pot. Glue clumps of moss and the crows on the arm and hat. Glue a 3" piece of the wire to back of remaining crow, insert in the pot.

SIGN PATTERN

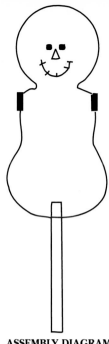

ASSEMBLY DIAGRAM

BIRD PATTERN

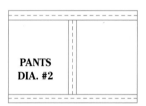

PANTS DIA. #1

PANTS DIA. #2

Basic Tips for Wood Dolls

Basecoat - Paint wood pieces with the indicated color. For smooth coverage use several thin coats of paint and a 3/4" paintbrush.

Eyes & **Mouth** - Dip the wood end of a liner brush in paint. Touch the end to the spot marked for the eye and lift. Repeat for the other eye. Use a Black or Red fine-tip permanent marker to draw the mouth.

Cheeks - Add blush to the cheeks with a swab. This will give the doll personality and 'life'.

Dot Letters - Use a permanent pen to draw letters. Make large dots on the ends of lettering.

Dress Dolls - Use muslin or calico. Rip fabric along the edges. Place the ripped edge on the pattern. Place pattern on folded fabric as indicated. Cut out fabric.

Sew Clothing - Machine stitch fabrics together with a 3/8" seam allowance. Use heavy duty craft thread and a large eye needle to sew a gathering stitch around the neckline and around the waist.

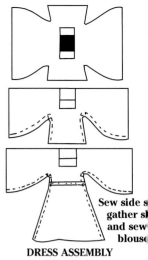

Sew side s
gather sl
and sew
blouse

DRESS ASSEMBLY
DIAGRAM

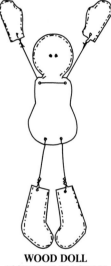

WOOD DOLL
ASSEMBLY DIAGRAM

Country at Heart

Twig wings float
around the
shoulders of this
country cutie.

Birdhouse Brenda *by Rochelle Norris*

WOOD PARTS: Doll body • 2 doll hands • 2 doll feet • 2 bird cutouts • Small chickadee chalet cutout • Small milk can cutout • ¾" button • 1½" flower pot

FABRIC: ⅓ yard of muslin for bloomers, ⅓ yard of Green plaid for dress, ¼ yard of Beige for apron

DECOART ACRYLIC PAINT: Mocha • Shading Flesh • Raw Sienna • Black • Buttermilk • Rookwood Red • Burnt Umber • Burnt Sienna • Antique Gold

MATERIALS:
Medium Brown looped mohair doll hair • Dried broom corn flowers • 10½" stick bow for wings • 1¼" wood screw • Screwdriver • Spanish moss • 2¼" and 3" pieces of cardboard • Craft wire • Cosmetic blush • cotton swab • Identi Pen

INSTRUCTIONS:

Doll - Cut the doll body from pine using the pattern. Basecoat the body and hands Mocha. Shade the face with Shading Flesh. Paint the feet Burnt Umber, dot Buttermilk. Rub the cheeks with blush. Draw the mouth, freckles and lines on hands with an Identi Pen. Assemble the doll using 15" of wire for the legs. Make the bloomers, put on the doll.

Dress - Tear two 6¾" x 13" pieces of dress fabric for the skirt. Make the dress, place on the doll. Sew thread through the button, tie a bow and glue on the neck.

Apron - Tear two 6¼" x 9½" pieces of apron fabric. With right sides together, sew around 3 sides. Turn right side out, iron. Hand stitch across top of the apron ½" from the top edges. Write 'every birdy Welcome' using an Identi pen, dot the letters. Paint the small birdhouse Burnt Umber, the roof Rookwood Red and the hole Black. Glue the birdhouse on the apron. Put the apron on the doll, pull threads tight around the waist, adjust the gathers and tie a knot.

Hair - For each bundle of hair, loosely wrap 2 strands around 2¼" cardboard 6 times. Remove from the cardboard and tie in the center with a piece of hair. Make 6 bundles. Glue 3 bundles on each side of the head. Wrap 2 strands of hair around 3" cardboard 6 times, tie with a strand of hair. Make 2 bundles. Glue on the top of the head. Tear a 1¼" x 10" strip of the Green plaid, tie a 2½" bow, glue on the hair.

Flowerpot - Wash the flower pot with Raw Sienna. Fill the pot with moss, glue to the inside of the hand. Glue the flowers in the pot.

Birds - Paint one bird Raw Sienna with Black details. Glue in the flower pot. Paint remaining bird Black with Antique Gold details. Glue a clump of moss on wings and bird on the moss.

Milk Can - Wash the can with Burnt Sienna. Write 'Bird seed' with an Identi Pen, dot the letters. Glue the can in place.

Wings - Center the wings on back of the doll. Attach with a wood screw. Thread a 5" piece of wire through the center of the bow for a hanger.

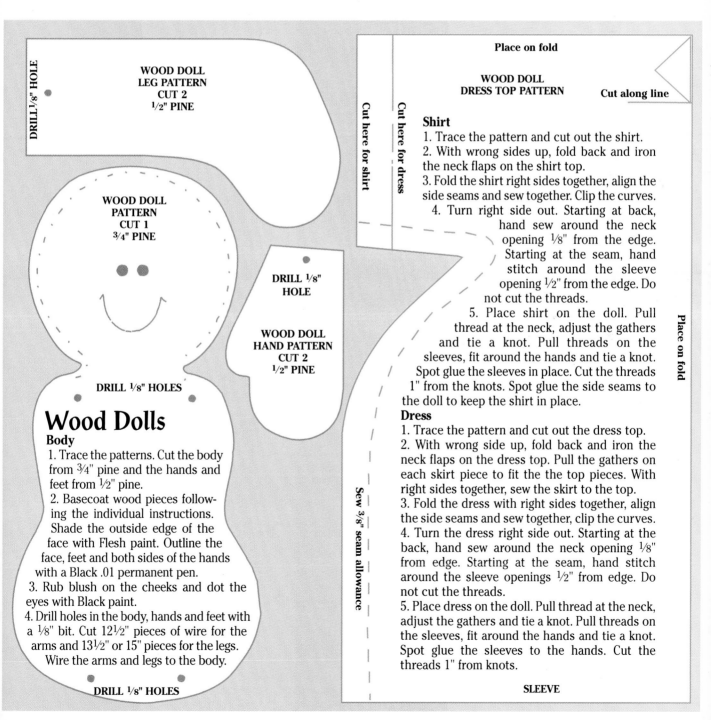

DRILL ⅛" HOLE

WOOD DOLL LEG PATTERN CUT 2 ½" PINE

Place on fold

WOOD DOLL DRESS TOP PATTERN

Cut along line

Cut here for shirt

Cut here for dress

WOOD DOLL PATTERN CUT 1 ¾" PINE

DRILL ⅛" HOLE

WOOD DOLL HAND PATTERN CUT 2 ½" PINE

DRILL ⅛" HOLES

Place on fold

Shirt

1. Trace the pattern and cut out the shirt.
2. With wrong sides up, fold back and iron the neck flaps on the shirt top.
3. Fold the shirt right sides together, align the side seams and sew together. Clip the curves.
4. Turn right side out. Starting at back, hand sew around the neck opening ⅛" from the edge. Starting at the seam, hand stitch around the sleeve opening ½" from the edge. Do not cut the threads.
5. Place shirt on the doll. Pull thread at the neck, adjust the gathers and tie a knot. Pull threads on the sleeves, fit around the hands and tie a knot. Spot glue the sleeves in place. Cut the threads 1" from the knots. Spot glue the side seams to the doll to keep the shirt in place.

Dress

1. Trace the pattern and cut out the dress top.
2. With wrong side up, fold back and iron the neck flaps on the dress top. Pull the gathers on each skirt piece to fit the the top pieces. With right sides together, sew the skirt to the top.
3. Fold the dress with right sides together, align the side seams and sew together, clip the curves.
4. Turn the dress right side out. Starting at the back, hand sew around the neck opening ⅛" from edge. Starting at the seam, hand stitch around the sleeve openings ½" from edge. Do not cut the threads.
5. Place dress on the doll. Pull thread at the neck, adjust the gathers and tie a knot. Pull threads on the sleeves, fit around the hands and tie a knot. Spot glue the sleeves to the hands. Cut the threads 1" from knots.

Sew ⅜" seam allowance

SLEEVE

Wood Dolls
Body

1. Trace the patterns. Cut the body from ¾" pine and the hands and feet from ½" pine.
2. Basecoat wood pieces following the individual instructions. Shade the outside edge of the face with Flesh paint. Outline the face, feet and both sides of the hands with a Black .01 permanent pen.
3. Rub blush on the cheeks and dot the eyes with Black paint.
4. Drill holes in the body, hands and feet with a ⅛" bit. Cut 12½" pieces of wire for the arms and 13½" or 15" pieces for the legs. Wire the arms and legs to the body.

DRILL ⅛" HOLES

Snow Buddy *by Rochelle Norris*

WOOD PARTS: Doll body • 2 doll legs • 3/16" thick bird cutout • 3/8" thick bird cut out • Birdhouse cut out • 1/2" thick large dome for base • Tall tree • 3" sign • 12" of 1/4 " dowel

FABRIC: 1/4 yard of Black/Brown check print for pants • 1/4 yard of Red plaid for shirt • 1 1/8" x 9" torn strip of Red plaid for bow

DECOART ACRYLIC PAINT: Light Buttermilk • Raw Sienna • Black • Hauser Dark Green • Burnt Orange • Yellow Ochre • Snow White

MATERIALS: Spanish moss • Medium weight jute • Man's Tan cotton sock • 6" and two 7 1/2" twigs • Cosmetic blush • Cotton swab • Sandpaper • Identi Pen

INSTRUCTIONS:

Doll - Cut the doll body from pine using the pattern. Drill 1/4" holes for arms. Basecoat the face Light Buttermilk, shade with Raw Sienna and spatter Black. Paint the feet Black, spatter Light Buttermilk. Dot the eyes and mouth Black. Rub the cheeks with blush. Paint the carrot nose Burnt Orange. Cut 15" leg wires, attach the legs to the body. Glue the stick arms and insert in the body.

Shirt - Make the shirt. Fold under bottom edges of the sleeves 1 1/4", hand stitch around the opening 1" from the folded edge. Put the shirt on the doll and gather around the neck. Tie fabric strip into a bow, glue on the neck.

Socks - Cut 2" off top of the Tan sock. Cut the 2" piece in half. With right sides together, sew the center back seams. Put the socks on the feet with the finished edges at the ankles.

Pants - Make the pants folding the bottom edge under 1/4" and hand stitching around the opening 1/8" from the folded edge. Put the pants on the doll, gather the legs around tops of the socks and tie a knot. Tie the waist in place. Make the straps using 1 1/4" x 9" strips of the pant fabric, glue on the pants.

Hat - Cut 4 1/2" piece off top of the Tan sock, roll up the bottom edge 2 times. Put the hat on head, spot glue in place. Fold 20" of craft thread in half, wrap around top of the hat and tie in a knot. Cut the ends to 2".

Base - Drill a hole in curve of the dome with 1/4" bit. Paint the base Snow White, spatter lightly with Black. Glue and insert the dowel in the hole. Squirt a small amount of glue on top of the shirt so glue runs to the center of the upper back. Push the top of the dowel into glue allowing the feet to touch the top of the base. Drill a hole in the front corner of the base using a 3/16" bit

Tree - Paint the tree Hauser Dark Green, sand lightly when dry and spatter Light Buttermilk.

Birdhouse - Paint the birdhouse Raw Sienna, the roof Hauser Dark Green and the hole Black. Make the stitches with a .01 pen and spatter Black. Glue the ends of 5" of jute to the back of the birdhouse for a hanger. Tie a jute bow, glue on the top of the birdhouse.

Birds - Paint the thick bird Black with Yellow Ochre details. Paint the thin bird Raw Sienna with Black details.

Sign - Paint the edge of the sign Raw Sienna brushing a little paint over the front edge. Write 'Please feed the Birds' and dot the letters with an Identi pen. Glue the stick to the back of the sign.

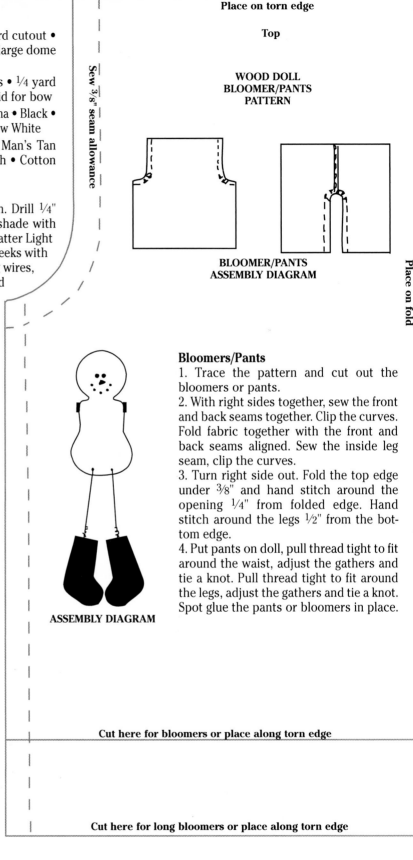

Place on torn edge

Top

WOOD DOLL BLOOMER/PANTS PATTERN

Sew 3/8" seam allowance

Place on fold

BLOOMER/PANTS ASSEMBLY DIAGRAM

ASSEMBLY DIAGRAM

Cut here for bloomers or place along torn edge

Cut here for long bloomers or place along torn edge

Bloomers/Pants

1. Trace the pattern and cut out the bloomers or pants.

2. With right sides together, sew the front and back seams together. Clip the curves. Fold fabric together with the front and back seams aligned. Sew the inside leg seam, clip the curves.

3. Turn right side out. Fold the top edge under 3/8" and hand stitch around the opening 1/4" from folded edge. Hand stitch around the legs 1/2" from the bottom edge.

4. Put pants on doll, pull thread tight to fit around the waist, adjust the gathers and tie a knot. Pull thread tight to fit around the legs, adjust the gathers and tie a knot. Spot glue the pants or bloomers in place.

Finish - Glue the tree to the front of the base and the moss to the tree. Hang the birdhouse from the arm. Glue the sign in the corner hole in the base and the thin bird on the sign. Glue moss around the stick. Glue moss on the shoulders and the Black bird on the moss.

'Please Feed the Birds'

All bundled up, the scarecrow is hardly a threat to birds. His sweet smile is more like a welcome to warm the soul during cold winter months.

Fabric Strips -
Rip or cut fabric into 1" x 44" strips using scissors or a rotary cutter.

Count Stitches -
Count stitches on the pattern. Count stitches on the rug canvas then mark the edges of the rug with a permanent marking pen.

Basic Instructions for Rag Rugs

Center Design -
Center the rug pattern on the canvas. Cut the canvas four threads larger than the pattern on all sides of the design. Turn the edges of the canvas under.

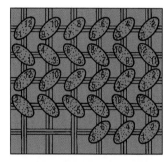

To finish a strip, run it under 3 stitches on the back of the rug. Cut off excess.

Stitch Design -
Work the design. Be sure to work the <u>Continental Stitch</u> by alternating the direction of each row... row 1 to the left, row 2 to the right, row 3 left, row 4 right, etc.

Stitch Border -
Make Whip Stitches around the border of the canvas going through both layers of canvas. Make 5 stitches in each corner. To begin stitching, hold 3" of fabric strip behind canvas and stitch over it.

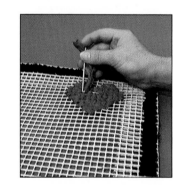

Stitch Background -
Work the colored background with Needlepoint Stitches. Be sure to work the <u>Continental Stitch</u> by alternating the direction of each row so the rug will stay 'square'.

Rag Rugs

When the first colonists arrived here from England, they brought with them only a few scraps of colored fabric. For making bed coverings, only a small colored or printed fabric piece was set in a window of coarse canvas, sacking or sail cloth to produce an interesting stained glass effect. Hence the name 'Cathedral' patchwork.

Stretching the life of fabrics has been carried down through the generations as women endured not only colonial times but also war and depression. Many a mother and grandmother will remember the short supply of all fabrics during these eras. Among their responsibilities, sewing clothes for the whole family and maintaining the home with linens, were among the most challenging.

So ingenious was my own mother that she took all my father's suits while he was away in the war, ripped them into strips and night after night used a large rug frame and a small hand hook to pull thousands of little bumps of fabric through a burlap backing until a gorgeous 9' x 12' rug was produced. The large floor covering was both practical and beautiful with a detailed floral design in the center surrounded by two oval rings of lacy green leaves.

Remembering my mother's diligence and the cumbersome frame that occupied a large chunk of space in our living room inspired me to invent a better way to make fabric rugs. By ripping fabric into strips and stitching the strips onto large-hole rug canvas, rag rugs are now much easier to make.

Some memories fade while others are woven so deeply into the soul that they can never be forgotten.

Honey 'Bee' Mine

'Bee' my little honey bee and I'll love you all the time. Buzz around, buzz around, buzz around.

Beehive and Honey Bees Rug

DESIGN SIZE: 18" x 24"
CANVAS: Canvas 78 holes wide x 58 holes high
44" WIDE FABRICS:

Design	Color	Number of 1" Strips	Yardage
Border	Brown Print	23	¾
Bee	Gold	5	¼
Wings	Ivory Print	3	⅛
Bee Trail	Tan Floral Print	2	⅛
Beehive Outline	Rust	6	¼
Beehive	Gold/Black Dot	12	⅜
Bee Stripes, Door	Black	9	⅜
Background	Blue Green	64	2

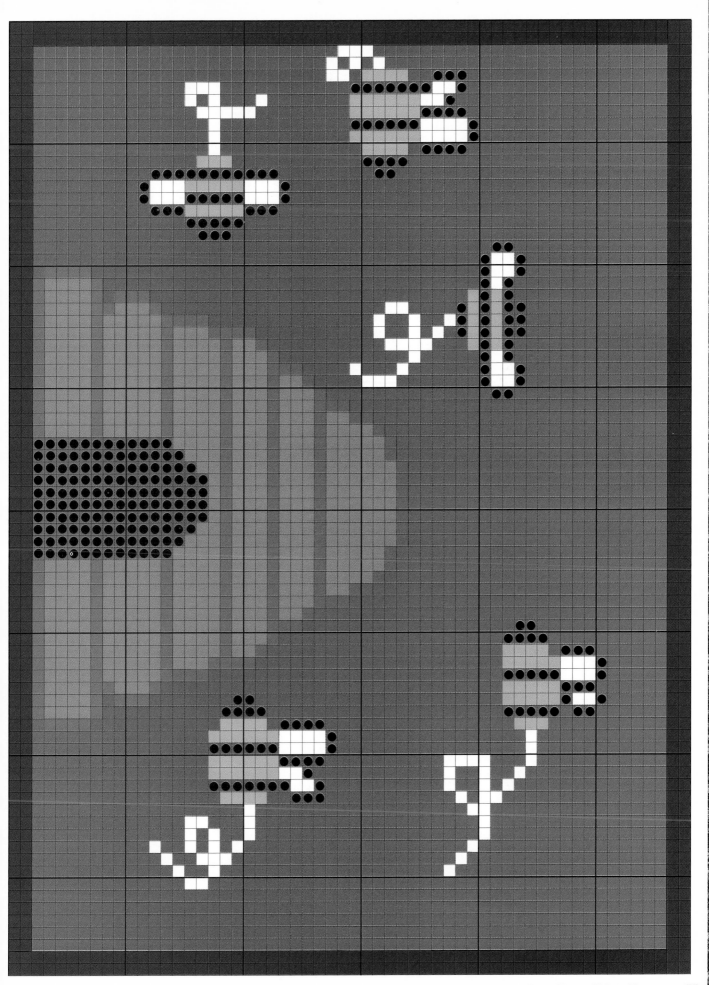

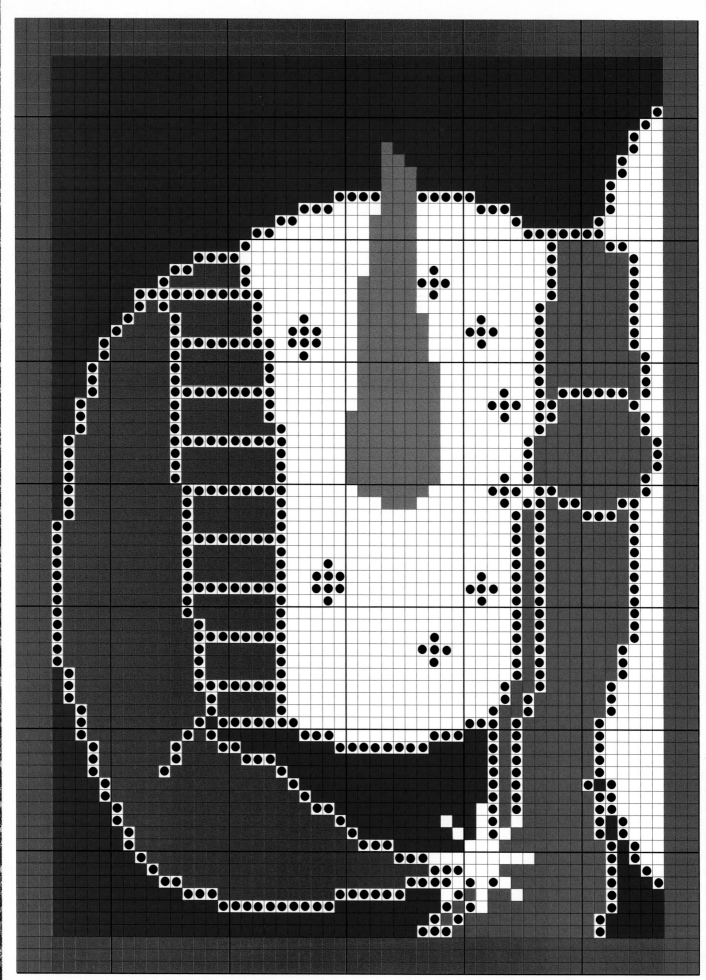

Big Snowman Face Rug

DESIGN SIZE: 18" x 24"
CANVAS: Canvas 78 holes wide x 58 holes high
44" WIDE FABRICS:

Design		Color	Number of 1" Strips	Yardage
Border		Mauve Print	29	1
Hat		Blue Print	17	⅝
Face, Snowflake		Ivory Print	20	⅝
Scarf		Dark Red Print	12	⅜
Details		Black	18	⅝
Nose		Gold Print	4	⅛
Background		Dark Green	29	1

Cheery Greeting

With a big smile made of coal
and a colorful carrot nose,
he will warm you inside and
keep the cold outside.

Log Cabin Hearts

Framed in memories, each heart is a symbol of the many ties that bind us to the past.

Framed Hearts Rug

DESIGN SIZE: 18" x 24"
CANVAS: Canvas 78 holes wide x 58 holes high
44" WIDE FABRICS:

Design	Color	Number of 1" Strips	Yardage
Hearts	Red	6	¼
Background	Brown	84	2⅝
Gold Stripes	Gold Print	11	⅜
Brown Stripes	Brown Print	8	¼
Teal Stripes	Teal	17	⅝
Green Stripes	Green	12	⅜
Blue Stripes	Blue Check	17	⅝

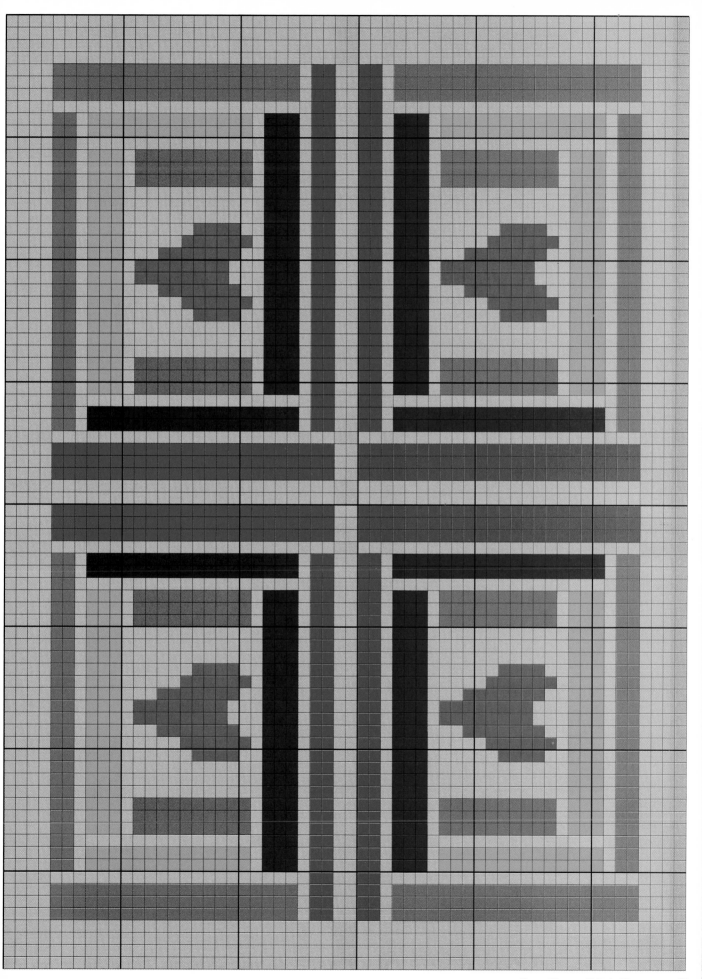

Welcome to 'Our' Home

A heartwarming welcome rug turns any house into a personalized home.

Personalized Welcome Rug

DESIGN SIZE: 18" x 24"
CANVAS: Canvas 78 holes wide x 58 holes high
44" WIDE FABRICS:

Design	Color	Number of 1" Strips	Yardage
Border	Green Check	39	1¼
Wavy Line	Dark Green	8	¼
Background	Beige Print	82	2⅝
Hearts, Name	Dark Red Print	17	⅝

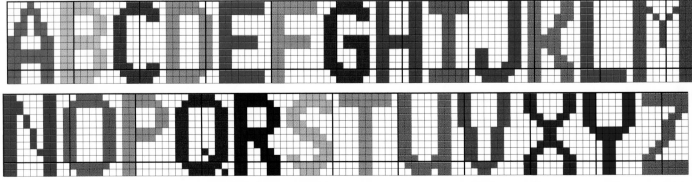

Use the alphabet to personalize your rug with your family name. Turn the M upside down to make a W.

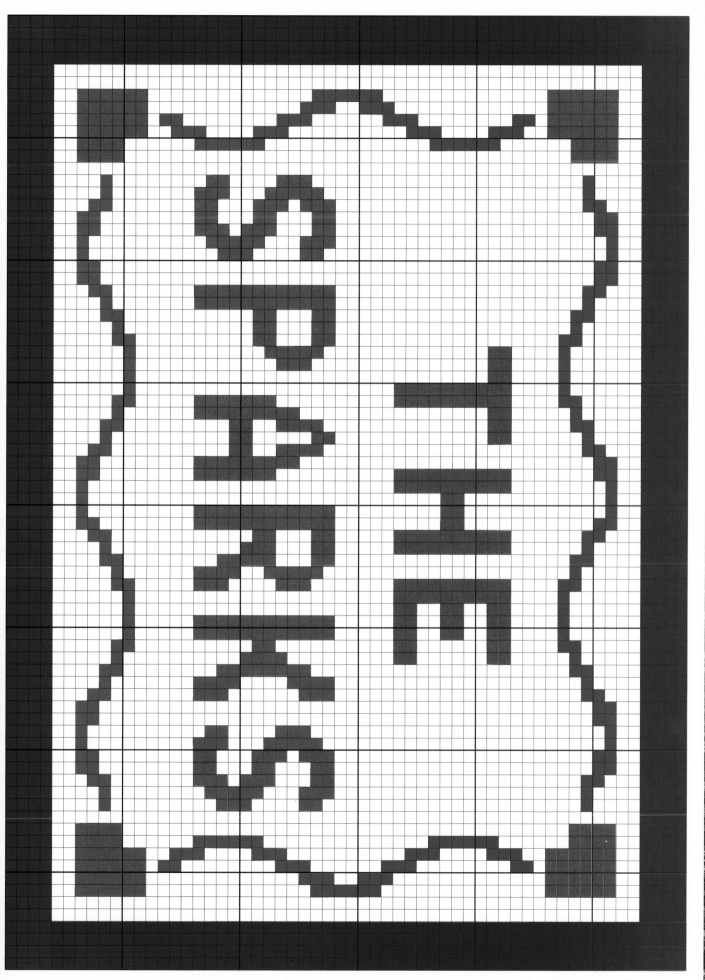

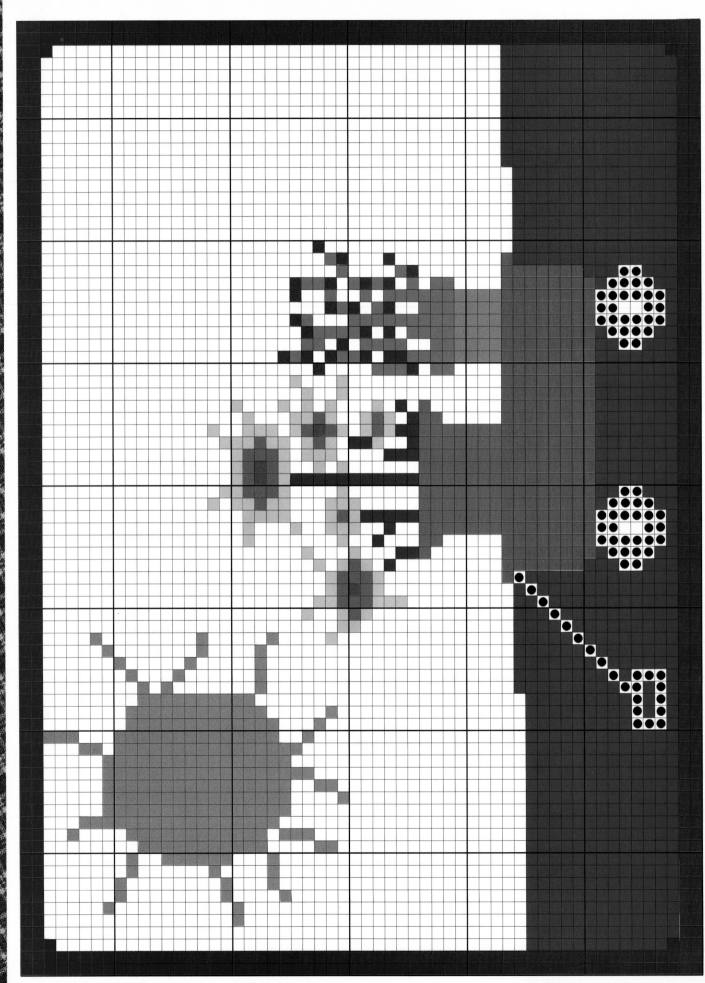

Red Wagon and Flowers Rug

DESIGN SIZE: 18" x 24"

CANVAS: Canvas 78 holes wide x 58 holes high

44" WIDE FABRICS:

Design		Color	Number of 1" Strips	Yardage
Border		Brown Print	21	¾
Sky		Light Blue Print	68	2⅛
Grass		Green Floral Print	24	¾
Wagon		Dark Red Print	6	¼
Wheels, Handle		Black	4	⅛
Wheel Centers		White	1	⅛
Sun		Gold Print	8	¼
Large Pot		Rust	2	⅛
Stems		Green	1	⅛
Flowers		Dark Red Print	1	⅛
		Blue Print	1	⅛
		Gold	1	⅛
Small Pot		Tan Print	1	⅛
Small Pot Rim		Gold/Black Dot	1	⅛
Flowers		Dark Blue Print	1	⅛
Vines		Dark Green	2	⅛

Sunshine and Flowers

**Waking up to sunny days
all summer long is guaranteed
with this cheerful flowering
rug under foot.**

Folk-Art Log House

Providing shelter from cold nights, sturdy log homes built by the pioneers kept families warm on the inside all winter long.

House Rug

DESIGN SIZE: 18" x 24"
CANVAS: Canvas 78 holes wide x 58 holes high
44" WIDE FABRICS:

Design		Color	Number of 1" Strips	Yardage
Border, Door Windows	■	Black	38	1¼
House Stripes	■	Beige Floral	17	⅝
	■	Brown Print	16	½
Roof	■	Green	7	¼
Window Frames Chimney Door Frames	■	Rust	7	¼
Tree Trunk	■	Brown/Gold	1	⅛
Tree	■	Dark Green	6	¼
Moon	■	Gold	3	⅛
Background	■	Blue Print	44	1¾
Grass	■	Green Floral	17	⅝

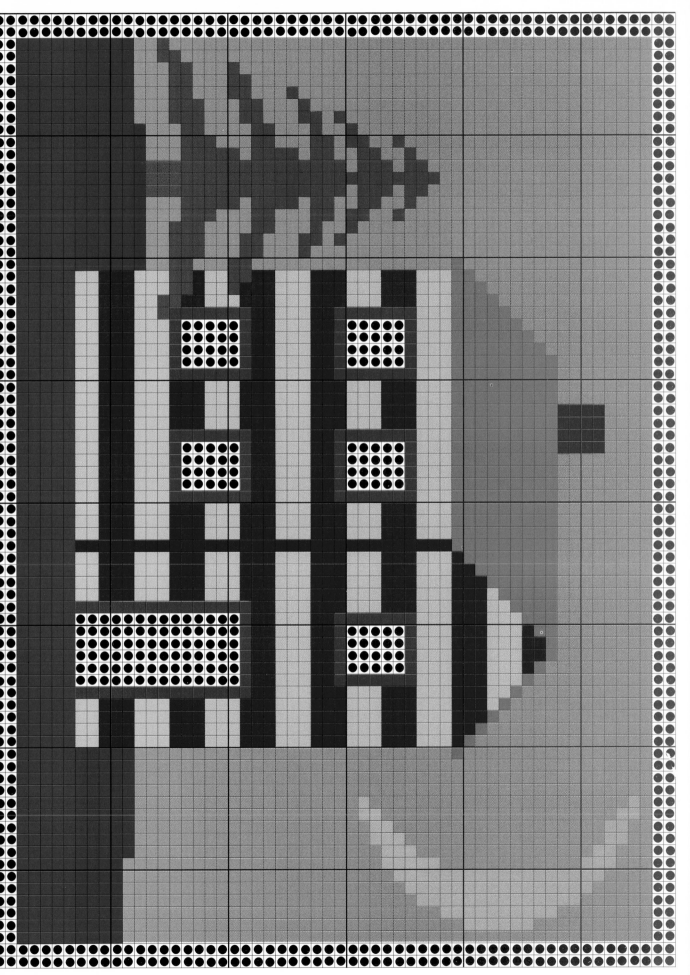

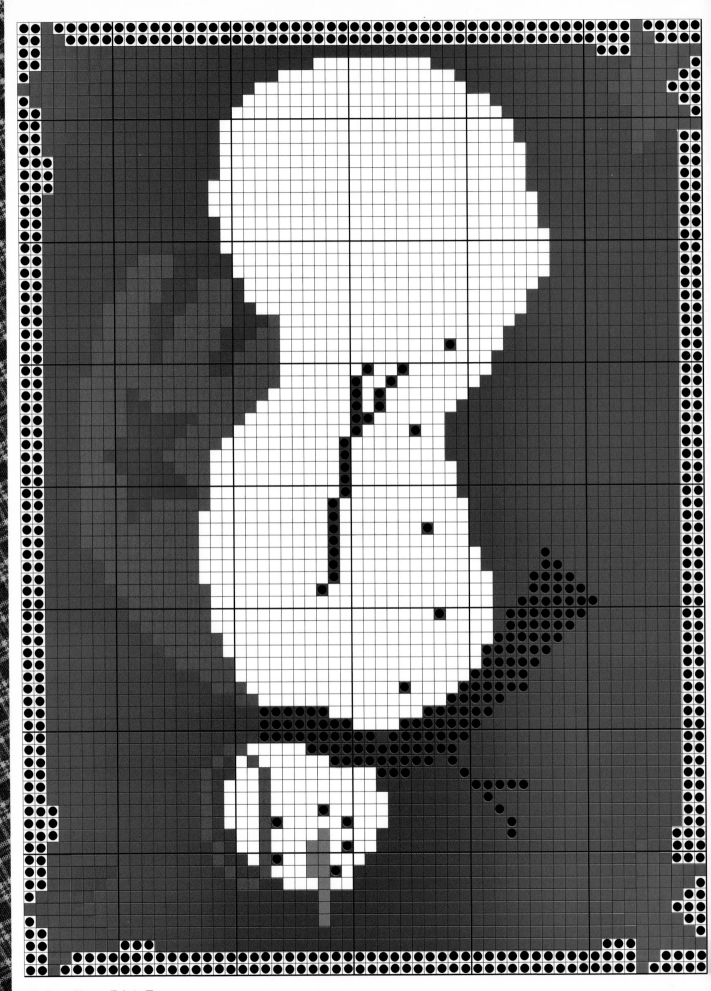

Flying Snowman Rug

DESIGN SIZE: 18" x 24"
CANVAS: Canvas 78 holes wide x 58 holes high
4" WIDE FABRICS:

Design		Color	Number of 1" Strips	Yardage
Border, Scarf				
Face, Details	■	Black	16	½
Snowman	□	Ivory Print	28	⅞
Wings, Halo		Dark Gold Print	10	⅜
Stars, Nose		Dark Red Print	7	⅜
Background		Blue	45	1½

Good Cheer Guardian

When the sun comes out, where does the snowman go? His soul floats up to the stars and he becomes a guardian of good cheer.

Angel on High

**Hark the herald,
Angels sing with
golden stars in the sky..**

Angel Rug

DESIGN SIZE: 18" x 24"
CANVAS: Canvas 78 holes wide x 58 holes high
44" WIDE FABRICS:

Design		Color	Number of 1" Strips	Yardage
Border		Blue Check	32	1
Trumpet		Gold Print	4	1/8
Dress		Dark Red Print	22	3/4
Wings		Gold/Black Dot	7	1/4
Highlights		Gold	2	1/8
Sleeve		Mauve	2	1/8
Face, Hand		Cream Print	2	1/8
Hair, Star		Brown Print	9	1/8
Collar		Burgundy	2	1/4
Background		Tan Print	65	2 1/8

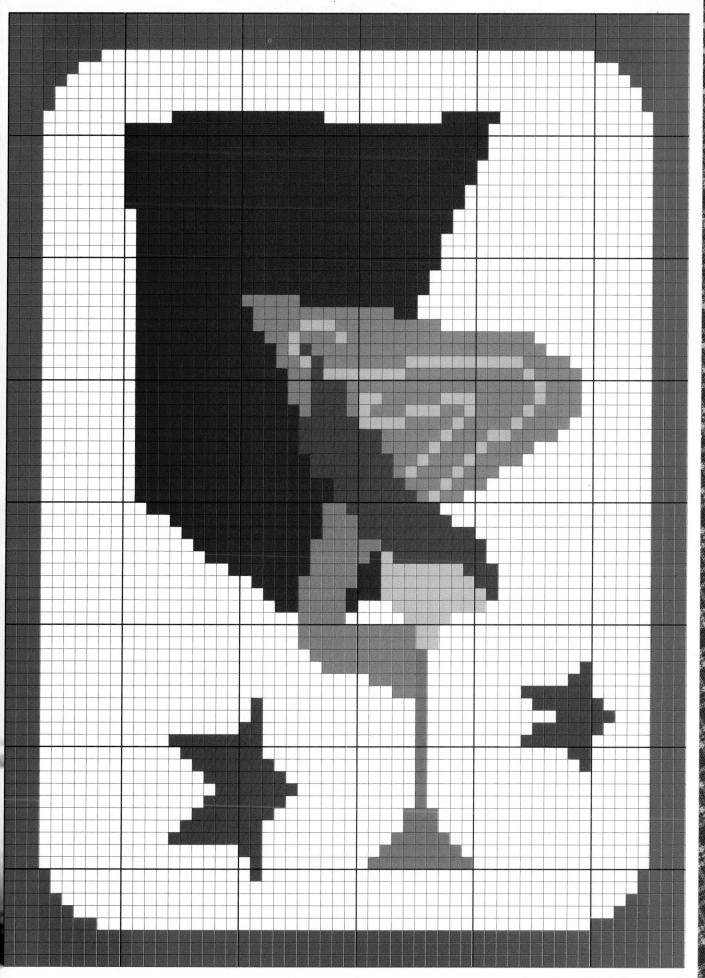

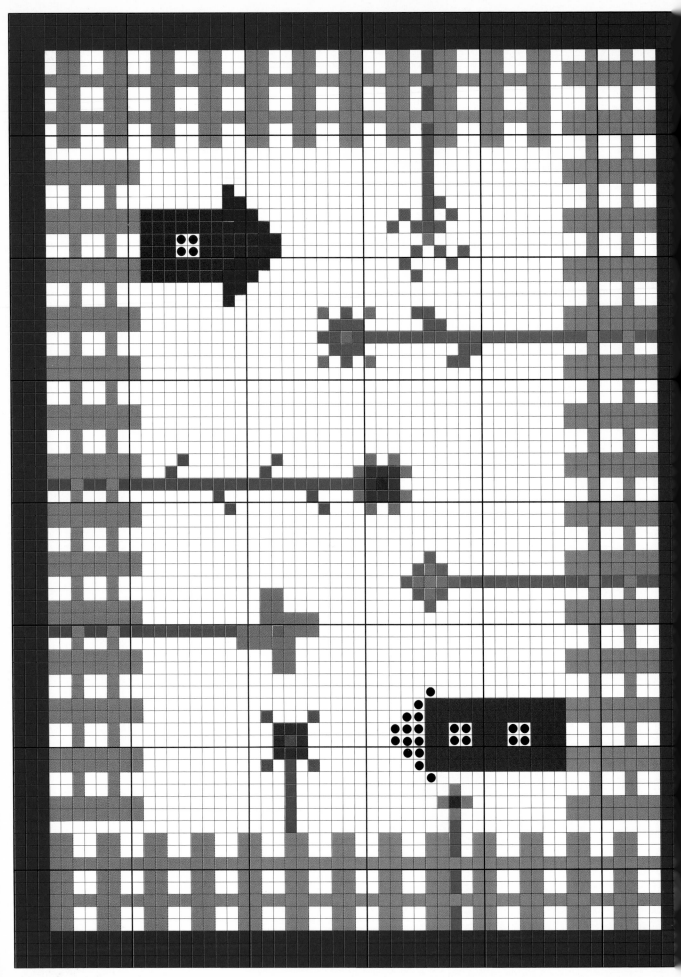

Birdhouses and Flowers Rug

DESIGN SIZE: 18" x 24"
CANVAS: Canvas 78 holes wide x 58 holes high
4" WIDE FABRICS:

Design		Color	Number of 1" Strips	Yardage
Border	■	Dark Green	31	1
Birdhouses 1, 2 Flowers	■	Blue Check	2	$\frac{1}{8}$
Birdhouse 2, Roof 1 2 Flower Centers	■	Brown Print	3	$\frac{1}{8}$
Roof 2, Holes	■	Black	2	$\frac{1}{8}$
Fence	■	Tan Check	33	$1\frac{1}{8}$
Stems, Leaves	■	Green	4	$\frac{1}{8}$
Flowers	■	Red Print	1	$\frac{1}{8}$
	■	Brown/Gold	1	$\frac{1}{8}$
	■	Dark Red	1	$\frac{1}{8}$
	■	Rust Print	1	$\frac{1}{8}$
	■	Blue Print	1	$\frac{1}{8}$
	■	Gold/Black Dot	1	$\frac{1}{8}$
Background	□	Ivory Print	67	$2\frac{1}{8}$

From the Garden

Welcome home where
there is a roof overhead,
a little picket fence, plenty
of singing birds and
flowers in the garden.

Heart to Heart

For this classic folk art design, our ancestors would have lovingly hand-dyed the reds, browns and greens using vegetables and even the earth's red clay for tints.

Six Hearts Folk-Art Rug

DESIGN SIZE: 18" x 24"
CANVAS: Canvas 78 holes wide x 58 holes high
44" WIDE FABRICS:

Design	Color	Number of 1" Strips	Yardage
Hearts	■ Dark Red Print	21	¾
Mat	■ Brown Print	38	1¼
Frame	■ Gold/Black Dot	31	1
Background	■ Green	48	1½